# Every Month Is August

## Loving a Child with Reactive Attachment Disorder and Navigating the Worlds of Education, Therapy, and Criminal Justice

### SHANNON FRIEND GILES

Every Month Is August © Copyright <<2021>> Shannon Giles

All rights reserved. No part of this publication may be reproduced, distributed or transmitted in any form or by any means, including photocopying, recording, or other electronic or mechanical methods, without the prior written permission of the publisher, except in the case of brief quotations embodied in critical reviews and certain other noncommercial uses permitted by copyright law.

Although the author and publisher have made every effort to ensure that the information in this book was correct at press time, the author and publisher don't assume and hereby disclaim any liability to any party for any loss, damage, or disruption caused by errors or omissions, whether such errors or omissions result from negligence, accident, or any other cause.

Adherence to all applicable laws and regulations, including international, federal, state and local governing professional licensing, business practices, advertising, and all other aspects of doing business in the US, Canada or any other jurisdiction is the sole responsibility of the reader and consumer.

Neither the author nor the publisher assumes any responsibility or liability whatsoever on behalf of the consumer or reader of this material. Any perceived slight of any individual or organization is purely unintentional.

The resources in this book are provided for informational purposes only and should not be used to replace the specialized training and professional judgment of a health care or mental health care professional.

Neither the author nor the publisher can be held responsible for the use of the information provided within this book. Please always consult a trained professional before making any decision regarding treatment of yourself or others.

For more information, email shannonfg88@gmail.com

ISBN: (E-book only) 978-1-7373862-0-9

ISBN: (print only) 978-1-7373862-1-6

To August, my firstborn, not of my body but of my heart. I'm so proud to be your mother and I love you beyond words. I'll always be your biggest fan.

*"A child born to another woman calls me Mom. The depth of the tragedy and magnitude of the privilege are not lost on me."*

- JODY LANDERS

# Table of Contents

# PREFACE

First of all, thank you for deciding to read my book. Secondly, if you're reading this book because you have a child like August, know that I understand how frustrated, scared, exhausted, and sad you may be feeling right now. And all those feelings are just fine.

No one goes into parenting planning for the challenges of raising a child with reactive attachment disorder. We all want the perfect picture we see on TV or in movies. But no family is perfect, even without the diagnosis of RAD. So, we suit up and face each day with love, humor, and maybe some modern pharmaceuticals if we choose, and we do our best. Because our best is all we have.

When you get to the end of this book, you might think that I think my parenting hasn't been as successful as it could have been. Or as you read it, you may think I've made mistakes along the way. Of course, I've made mistakes! Tons of them! No one gets through parenting without screwing up something. And with RAD, it's doubled. And then double that. And then tripled on top of that! There's no road map for RAD just like there's no road map for parenting any child.

What I hope you get from reading this book is that I went into parenting August with my eyes open and my heart full, that I did everything I could to learn about his disorder and find him the best care I could, that I made tough choices that broke my heart but which I did out of love, and that never, NEVER did I give up.

And this book is just the beginning. Sign up for emails at my website and you'll get free checklists that will help you with your own journey with your "radish" (a term you might see when referring to kiddos with RAD on social media).

These will be explored more fully in future *Every Month is August* books and, on my blog, which you can find at www.everymonthisaugust.com

## CHAPTER ONE

# *Finding August*

always assumed I'd have children. I think a lot of us do that when we're little. We dream of growing up, getting married, and having children. I was no different. I got married a little late at 28 years old, so my biological clock wasn't ticking loudly, but I could certainly hear it!

After about a year, we began "trying." Isn't it supposed to be fun?" Well, the "fun" stopped pretty fast when it became apparent that something wasn't working. Having a baby is much less romantic when it involves doctors and nurses, shots, blood draws, egg retrieval, sperm donations, and embryo transfers. I don't want to dwell too much on this part of the story because this isn't what this book is about except that it does explain how much August was wanted when we got to the point of adoption. But after ten rounds of IVF—thank you, state of Massachusetts for mandating insurance coverage for infertility!—and many rounds of IUIs and other fertility medications that were all unsuccessful, I was despondent.

After seven years of trying, I was 35 years old. We moved twice and were living in Portland, Oregon. We had an amazing circle of friends but were far away from family. We both had good jobs and were making a lot of money. Oregon is a wonderful place for camping and hiking. It's an amazing wine producing state, and going to wineries for wine tasting is a great time. We really could have been very happy with our lives, but there was a hole that only a child could fill. And that still wasn't happening.

So, we made the decision to start looking into adoption. I knew I wanted to be a mom, even if it meant not giving birth. As we saw it, we had three options: private infant adoption, adoption through the state foster care system, or international adoption. August's dad wasn't crazy about foster care adoption. I wasn't keen on it but was maybe more desperate. We had taken classes to learn about that process, and they do a great job in trying to scare you to death with what those children have been through. And then they try and scare you more with what behaviors may result from that abuse. Little did I know that what I'd be dealing with down the road might be as bad or so much worse.

I wasn't crazy about private infant adoption. I couldn't get my brain around the fact that I would always feel like a long-term babysitter. Most private adoptions are open and it just didn't seem right to be "watching" someone's child that I'd have to report to. Sending pictures and letters to let someone know how I was raising "her" child just didn't sit right with me. I know that's not how it actually works but that's how it worked in my head. So that option was out.

For both of us, the second choice was international adoption. So that's where we landed. We began the process in the fall of 2000. We selected an adoption agency based in the Northwest for obvious ease of use, and it had a great reputation. We dove into the paperwork, which made buying a house seem simple. There was nothing about our lives that wasn't scrutinized. Our income, our health, our home, our families, everything was picked over. We had to write individual personal stories in which we lay bare our lives, including why adopting a child and becoming a parent was so important to us. That was so important and so beneficial because it really allowed me the first opportunity to stop and sit with myself and analyze why I was going down this road and what I was expecting to find at the other end. I imagine if I had put down in my story the parenting experiences I was about to go through (like I am now), I might never have met August!

Then there was another sheet of paper, a list of all the possible conditions our future child could have that we would be willing to accept. It was truly the most depressing thing I had ever had to do. It listed things like missing limbs, cleft palate, deaf, paraplegic, and a variety of lesser issues as well. How do you do this? How do you pick what you'd be willing to accept in a child? If you were having a child, you wouldn't get such a luxury. And now after seven years of wanting children so desperately, the temptation to take any child no matter what the issue was hard to resist. But in thinking about it, I realized that this may be the only child we have, and now is the time to be selfish. After seven years, we needed to be very aware of our limitations and not take on more than we knew we were able just because we were so desperate to be parents. This was never more evident than when the agency presented us with a child who obviously had severe issues. Fetal Alcohol Syndrome and a host of developmental delays. Despite our desperation to be parents, we knew it was more than we could handle and passed. Once again, little did we know how much we were about to take on!

Adopting from Russia is a moving target. The rules change frequently. We got caught up in that during our adoption process. The rule allowing for adoption agencies to begin the process on behalf of families was changed and then only adoption agencies that were certified could still petition for their families. While our agency in Seattle was wonderful, they didn't get certified due to a paperwork problem, so we found ourselves having to change agencies and redo all our paperwork six months into the process. It was awful but we loved the new agency, and they were in Raleigh, where we used to live, which we took as a good sign.

The paperwork was redone, notarized, apostilled—when

the notarization is verified by the Secretary of State—and compiled into a complete dossier which was sent to the agency. That was in February of 2001. About a month later, we got a call from the agency. Now, here's the interesting part. One of the other things we had to decide was the age of the child. First, we decided we wanted a child under two. At the last minute, we changed our request to under three. When the call came, they were concerned because the child they wanted us to take a look at had just turned three a week earlier, on March 22, 2001. We said we would be willing to take a look. A week wasn't much of a difference.

By FedEx in a day came our first introduction of August. There was a picture of him sitting in very ornate wing chair. He had a serious and scared look on his face and piercing blue eyes that conveyed a life of experience much more than his three little years. He was wearing a decorative red jumper with white tights and red low-cut, flat-soled shoes with a button strap. It looked like a costume for Octoberfest. Along with the photo was a couple of pages that outlined his brief medical and family history. There wasn't much except he'd lived with his biological mother until he was two and then he was removed from her care and placed in the orphanage. It listed his height, weight and head circumference numbers and a bunch of other information from various doctors who had checked him out.

But then there was a video. We saw him running, walking, talking, smiling, and laughing. And we watched it over and over again. Within a few minutes of viewing the video, he was my son. It's hard to put into words how I made the connection with August through the television. I looked into his eyes; I heard his voice. I saw his smile and everything about him told me he was my son. Just as much as if he'd been newly born and placed on my stomach in a delivery room.

But having a video and having him in my arms were very far apart. There was some due diligence to do and still much more paperwork to cross the ocean. We got the name of a doctor in Seattle who was an expert in interpreting the information about a child that comes with the referral to let us know if there were any red flags we should consider. She looked at his medical history that was sent, and what she said was surprising. She said she was amazed that he was alive. Based on his initial height, weight, and head circumference numbers when he was brought to the orphanage, she wouldn't have expected him to survive because he was so developmentally delayed. He had made remarkable progress in the year he'd been at the orphanage to catch up, though he was still quite delayed on all three measurements. But she said he was obviously a resilient little boy. That was going to be realized on so many occasions over the following years, as we would come to see.

Within a week, we had accepted the referral of August as our adopted son and made the decision to move forward. The waiting to get a court date in Russia had begun. Oh, and I should mention that his home was in Monchegorsk, a small town in the Murmansk region of Russia next to Finland and 125 miles north of the Arctic Circle, not the most pleasant place to grow up.

About six weeks later, the call came. Friday, May 4th. Life couldn't have been more chaotic. My company had been bought by a competitor. I had laid off half of my staff and was in the process of moving my remaining staff and office into the competitor's office in downtown Portland. My mood wasn't good. So, when the call came that day that we'd be traveling to Russia right before Memorial Day to finalize

August's adoption, it was the most joyous moment of my life. Everything got real, really fast. It took some time to get my brain around the fact that in three weeks, I would be August's mother.

But the weekend of chaos wasn't over. I hadn't been paying much attention to things while all of the office moved and the stress related to that was happening. I just wanted to get the merger done and I was desperate to get that all-important Friday call. However, it did cross my mind on Saturday of that weekend that I couldn't remember the last time I'd gotten my period. Because I definitely had bigger issues to focus on, after church on Sunday, we bought a pregnancy test just so I could take it, know I wasn't pregnant, and move on. But it was positive. Oops.

We sat for about an hour in the family room just digesting what had happened in the last 48 hours. Friday morning, we had no children. By Sunday at noon, we were going to have two. As I've said many times, I wouldn't change it but I don't recommend it. The stress level went nuclear. We had a lot to do in that short three weeks. Travel visas, plane tickets, clothes for August, some more paperwork, arrangements with our jobs and families. Oh yes, and a trip to the doctor to confirm that I was, in fact, pregnant.

Then, on May 24th, 2001, we were headed to Russia.

CHAPTER TWO

*Meeting August*

Landing in Moscow was just as surreal as I imagined it would be. I've traveled internationally before. But never to a country where not only did I not know the language, but I didn't even know the alphabet. Plus, we weren't exactly sure who was meeting us there. Luckily, we were met by a lovely woman who would be with us constantly as an interpreter. We also had a driver because no one drives themselves in Moscow.

We loaded our luggage, and several boxes of donated items we had brought for a group our church worked with and headed for the hotel. Turns out we were staying at a Marriott. Just a plain, regular Marriott. From the inside, if you didn't hear anyone speak, we could have been in Atlanta. There was a sign advertising that the Eagles would be coming later that month. We checked in, got to our room, and immediately fell asleep. I'm not even sure I knew what day or time it was.

When we woke up, August's dad wanted to go wander around. We weren't too far from Red Square, so we walked up there. I was already beginning to have morning sickness, after finding out I was more pregnant than I thought I was. I sat on some steps and enjoyed the scenery for a while. It was so incredible to see St. Peter's and the Kremlin, buildings that for years I'd seen in pictures associated with communism and oppression. August's dad had been out earlier and said he was terrified of going too far from the hotel because he imagined an unmarked van coming by and scooping him up, never to be seen again. Our impressions of old Russia still lingered despite all the changes that had taken place over the decades. And it never really subsided the entire time we were there. There were a McDonald's and a TGI Friday's very near our very American looking hotel but otherwise, we were totally out of our element. And we didn't know how much worse it was about to get.

The next day, we were scheduled to leave for the Murmansk region where Monchegorsk was located. The Murmansk region's capital city was also called Murmansk. It was a strategic port city during World War II because even that far north, the port didn't freeze. Monchegorsk didn't have any claims to fame however. The guidebook said, "If you ever had a notion of visiting Hell, Monchegorsk is a good place to start." And this was from a book that was trying to convince us to travel there! Monchegorsk had been the site of a nickel smelting plant and had suffered from years of unchecked toxic emissions from the plant. The land was considered uninhabitable. I couldn't get my brain around what that meant, but it was fairly obvious when we arrived.

Our flight to Murmansk was aboard a regional Russian airline and we were upgraded to first class by our Russian traveling companion, David. He was a great guy, full of life and energy. Prior to coming into the adoption business, he'd been an oil rigger off the coast of Azerbaijan. Quite the change in careers! He took great care of us, getting us to the airport and onto the plane. By the way, *us* was now a foursome. We were now traveling with another couple from Raleigh, NC who were going to the same town to adopt a seven-year-old little girl. They were a sweet couple, and it was wonderful to have others with whom to share our experience.

We landed in Murmansk at about 12:30 am local time. It was still light out and snowing. Remember that we are north of the Arctic circle and it's the end of May. This was an excellent setting of the stage for the beginning of our surreal adventure in the Murmansk region. We had a new driver who took us to our hotel. The town of Murmansk was very industrial and commercial. We didn't drive through neighborhoods. We saw a glimpse of the port for which Murmansk was famous. Even though it's so far north, it has a bizarre current that keeps it from freezing. Just prior to our arrival, a submarine had sunken in the port, and the crew had been lost. It definitely looked very different from anything in the United States.

The hotel wasn't anything luxurious. That's probably no surprise. There was a bedroom and a separate sitting area, which would come in handy later. And a bathroom with hot and cold running yellow water. That wasn't reassuring. A restaurant was in the lobby. One of the spooky parts of being in Russia is that when you stay at a hotel, they keep your passport while you stay there. I suppose it's so you can't skip out on the bill. But surrendering my passport wasn't a comfortable thing to do.

The next morning was it, the day I got to meet August. The restaurant was the only place to eat and featured eggs, some sort of boiled chicken, a congealed rice, and kefir. Kefir is a buttermilk-type beverage that's thicker than milk but thinner than yogurt. Much of what's served in Russia is room temperature other than coffee. And nothing is pasteurized. Since I was pregnant, food choices were complicated both from a baby health standpoint and from a morning sickness standpoint. Luckily this was pre-9/11, and I was able to pack a backpack full of Snackpack puddings and granola bars. That was my salvation for the entire trip!

We climbed in something like a VW bus and headed out. It was about a two-hour drive down to Monchegorsk, which was south of the city of Murmansk. The road—if you could call it that—was a series of potholes held together with some tar. And the shocks on the bus weren't working very well. I looked out the window trying to keep my stomach calm from both the morning sickness and the nerves that were churning at the prospect of meeting August. Pulling into Monchegorsk, the surroundings revealed all the information the guidebook and the Internet had described.

We saw rundown buildings, both homes and businesses. Old tires were strewn about along with the remains of cars and machines. We didn't see much evidence of a vibrant economy or of a vibrant anything. We finally arrived at the orphanage. It was a nondescript building with an old metal swing set outside. Since it had snowed, we couldn't see if there was any grass, but I doubted it. We walked inside and the first thing that struck me was how bright and cheery the place was. Murals were painted on the clean white walls. And everything was neat and well-cared for.

We met the orphanage director. She was a lovely woman who looked just like you'd want an orphanage director to look. A middle-aged, slightly overweight woman with colored blond hair and a big smile. We also met Yuri, who would also be facilitating our adoption along with David. He looked exactly like you'd imagine a Russian soldier to look, which made sense, since he used to be in the Russian Navy. He had shocking black hair, a bushy mustache, and a long heavy wool coat. But he was a favorite of the children, which was such a fun thing to watch. And we met the director's daughter who would serve as our interpreter so that our Moscow interpreter could go with our traveling companions to the other orphanage to meet their daughter. After the meetings, they were off. I didn't have much time to register that a town as small and sad as Monchegorsk had *two* orphanages.

The next thing that happened changed my life forever. As we were standing there, in he came. He was wearing the same outfit he'd been wearing in the video: a red short jumper with a white shirt under, white tights and red leather shoes that had a button strap. He held the hand of the director, and tucked himself slightly behind her leg. He had a round face with huge blue eyes. That's the thing I remember the most. Those eyes. Full of hope, fear, and curiosity. The director was speaking to him in Russian and I kept hearing her say, "Mama" and "Papa." After a minute, she pulled his hand toward me. I had more butterflies than I thought possible. I have them now just remembering that moment. I had come prepared with a way to break the language barrier with something that spoke the universal language of boys: I held out a Hot Wheels car. He quickly came toward me to take the car and looked at it. He knew exactly what it was and what to do with it. He was still shy and withdrawn, but the ice had been broken.

We proceeded to take a tour of the orphanage, led by the director. August came along and was very lively as we went to the various parts of the building. We went into a classroom, and she showed us how he was learning his letters (in Russian, of course). We went into a playroom and August played in a ball pit, which was obviously a favorite! They had a music room and a room where they made crafts that they sold. It was a lovely place really. Afterwards, we went back to her office and had tea, very strong, loose leaf tea. August stayed for a bit, then left to go to his class. We discussed how August was doing, some broader understanding of the orphanage, and how it runs.

After a couple hours, it was time to leave. We went back in to where the children were. August was in a circle with eight or so other children. When we went in, they all started calling us "Mama" and "Papa." We got to see where they slept which was a large room with small beds barely larger than the children all lined up in rows. I don't know how they got so many children asleep all together in one room like that. And tables were set up for lunch with real china tea cups filled with hot tea and matching plates, nicer than I ever use when I eat!

We stopped at a restaurant in town for lunch. In Russia, vodka is a condiment. It's on the table and it's available pretty much every meal. It was very hard to politely decline and not feel rude. They did serve a delicious stew/soup, which was very welcome on the snowy and cold day. And in 2001, the bathroom was a hole in the floor. The bumpy hour-and-a-half ride back to the hotel was full of reflection for me. I had just met my son. How surreal! Leaving him was so hard, even though I'd only known him for two hours, and I already couldn't wait to get back there.

The next day, we bumped our way back to Monchegorsk. August seemed happy to see us, still wearing his red jumper and white tights. I had thought maybe those were just his clothes for formal occasions, but it seemed like they were, in fact, all he had. We were informed that we'd have to send clothes down for him to wear after court when he was brought back up to us. The visit was pretty much the same as the day before, minus the tour. They served us tea and we got to play with August. The rides down and back were bumpy and anxious. We ate at the same restaurant with the vodka on the table and the hole-in-the-floor toilets. That was the last visit before he would become our son.

Monday was Memorial Day in the United States. On the other side of the world, it was court day. Court was held in Murmansk where we were staying, so no more bumpy van rides. We only had to wait a few hours until we went across the street to the government building. After the fall of the Soviet Union, the independent Russian country had a lot more government buildings than it needed. This was a complex of a few rundown buildings that definitely showed the glory of a bygone time. Statues and large impressive staircases led to large impressive buildings but now were slowly degrading and all but abandoned.

We went into one of the buildings and were shocked to see desks stacked up in the hallways of an almost completely deserted space. We walked to the end of a hallway to a room that functioned as the courtroom. Our fellow traveling family had gone before us, so we waited until they were finished. When it was our turn, we went into the room. The judge sat to our left. I was surprised to see it was a woman. We sat with our interpreter and the woman who was our "attorney" at a table on the opposite side of the room. At a table perpendicular to ours was a woman who served as the "prosecutor." Her job was to ensure that we were fit to adopt and that August was legally free for adoption. I automatically felt guilty. As the proceedings began, all in Russian, it was all mostly formalities. But after that, our attorney started talking about August and that's when my heart broke.

She explained that he was born to a girl of 16 years old. No father was identified, as it was thought the girl was a prostitute. There was no evidence of prenatal care. She was living with her mother at the time and continued to live with her for the first two years of his life. At that time, her mother moved South to Georgia. With no reliable assistance, she started leaving August with friends or neighbors when she went out, sometimes days at a time. Eventually, a neighbor called the Russian version of Social Services because he'd been alone in their apartment for several days. He was removed from his mother and placed in the hospital because he had pneumonia. He stayed there for a month, after which he was placed in the orphanage. His birth mother didn't want him back, and, upon contacting his birth grandmother,

her only question was if she also got the apartment if she took him. The answer must have been no because she didn't agree to take him. Both of their rights were terminated, and he was free to be adopted.

We were only asked a few questions. Were we willing to preserve his Russian heritage? Would he have his own room? What relatives would he have? More formalities in Russian and then it was over. The whole thing took maybe a half hour. At the end, the judge granted us the adoption. It was in Russian, so we got it through the interpreter. It was kind of anticlimactic that way. Then we had to appeal to the prosecutor to waive the 10-day waiting period required in Russia before any court decisions could be made effective. It meant that we couldn't leave the country with August for 10 more days. Luckily, they agreed to the waiver. The court appearance was over. We were parents.

The next two days were spent getting paperwork done: a new birth certificate listing us as parents and release of August's passport (in Russia no one holds their passport). This is where all the gifts and cash we had brought came into play. Only the fathers and the handlers went into the records offices and walked right by all the very long lines of people and got things processed very quickly. We stopped asking what the money and gifts did. We knew it wasn't exactly legal, but it made things easier for us.

On Thursday, the orphanage brought the children up. Our traveling companions had adopted a seven-year-old girl with blond hair and blue eyes. When they got to the hotel, it was lunchtime, and we went to the restaurant. Both the children could eat! August ate like he hadn't eaten in a month. With no concern for what was on the plate, he just shoveled it all in. We had to go get his picture taken for his INS card and then it was just us. I didn't expect it to be so awkward to be alone with August, but he was still a stranger and, oh yeah, we didn't speak Russian!

We gave him a bath in the room, which he loved. We didn't have any place for him to sleep so we got extra sheets and blankets and made him a bed on the loveseat in the outer room of our room and pushed chairs against it so he wouldn't fall. The loveseat was too small for either his dad or me to sleep on. I'm not sure any of us slept.

Friday, we flew back to Moscow. I expected August to be afraid of the plane trip but he was fascinated by everything! Buttons to push, more food, being in the air; he was thrilled. We got back to the Marriott and went to a Friday's restaurant. Trying to order food for a child we can't speak with and give an order to a waiter we can't speak with was an adventure! But as we'd learned, he wasn't very picky. After dinner came another bath. That's when we discovered his laugh. When he was little, he had the most amazing laugh. And hearing that was pure joy, even with not being able to communicate one word with him.

The next day, we packed up to leave. We were driven to the airport where we waited in a horrendously long line just to check in. The inbound flight was going to be late, so everyone was going to miss their connections, so they were trying to rebook everyone as they checked in. Just what we wanted when we're traveling with a three-year-old we just met. We spent two hours in a line with a ton of luggage, nothing to do, nowhere to go, and no ability to communicate. We finally got through that line and queued up to go through customs. We were in that one for several hours as well. And where was all the food? Yep. On the other side. Amazingly enough, August was a trooper. He sat quietly on top of the luggage while we got checked in and then waited much more patiently as we endured the long line in customs. We eventually got through customs and were able to get some food. And then we boarded the one flight from Moscow to JFK Airport in New York. Because now we were flying with a child with a Russian passport and there were only two other countries we could fly through with August: England and The Netherlands. So, we had to get this one flight. It's called the baby flight because all parents and newly adopted children take it.

The flight was 13 hours. All the advice we got said that now was not the time to try to be a good parent. If your child wasn't sleeping, drug them. We'd brought Benadryl. And after all those hours in the airport, we needed him to sleep. Plus, we couldn't get him to stop messing with all the buttons on the plane! The Benadryl goes in and we wait. Nothing happens. In fact, he gets more energetic. Apparently, we have the child who gets the "may cause excitability" side effect of Benadryl. How was I to know? This would be an important piece of information in later years, but right then, it just sucked. For about five hours of the flight, I held my child in the galley of the plane and tried unsuccessfully to rock him to sleep while standing so, at least, his dad could get a little sleep.

When we arrived in New York, we had to go through immigration with August, so that burned some time. Then customs, luggage, and we finally got to our hotel where we had all of four hours to sleep before we had to be back up and rush back to the airport for our flights home. We couldn't get a direct flight to Portland, so we have to go through Salt Lake City. I had enough frequent flyer miles, so I upgraded us all to first class. It was totally selfish because I wanted to have a bathroom I didn't have to share with as many people. It proved to be a smart move because I threw up five times on the flights home.

At long last, we made it home. A good friend picked us up, and while I'd hoped for a great moment when August saw his forever home, he fell asleep on the ride. After 23 hours of travel, it was about time! But he woke up for us to get him in the house and show him his room. I barely remember the rest of that day because we were all so tired from the flights. But that night, June 4, 2001, August slept in his bed in his room in our house as my son.

## CHAPTER THREE

# And they lived happily ever after...

Oh, how I wish I could write those words and have that be the end of my story. But, of course, it was just the beginning. We did have a lovely honeymoon period. I have such a sweet memory of the first Sunday we walked into church. We were late because we weren't used to having to get a three-year-old ready along with ourselves! And church had started. The associated pastor was doing announcements when we walked in the back doors and she saw us. She had the most calming voice and she very quietly told the congregation that we were there. The entire church turned around and looked. So many smiles and a few tears. It was just beautiful. I waved and held August's hand up and waved to give him the idea that he should wave (I had no idea what the Russian word for wave was!) He waved! And the entire congregation waved back with a united, "Ahhhh!"

August's dad had a generous paternity leave which allowed us to have several weeks to get settled in. We had learned some Russian with which we could get through the day, handling the big issues like food, bathroom, bedtime, and, "I love you!" We made a trip to the beach which proved to be very revealing. We knew there was no way he'd ever seen the ocean. But he absolutely loved it. We couldn't get him out of the water. And the Pacific Ocean in Oregon in June is COLD! One of my favorite pictures of August shows him with blue lips, blue fingernails, and visible goosebumps but a huge smile!

In January our family had another big change, the addition of August's little brother. My advice to anyone who might continue to try to have a biological child while pursuing adoption and hears my story of getting two kids in seven months is, "Wouldn't change it, don't recommend it." I can credit August with having a much healthier pregnancy than I would have had otherwise. After seven years of infertility, I would have been tempted to sit on a couch for nine months once I found out I'd gotten pregnant. August certainly meant that wouldn't be happening. I was swimming, running around, hiking, and rolling around on the floor, so there was no time to worry!

But I saw some indications of things to come in how August reacted to his brother's arrival. They may have been typical for an older sibling but, in hindsight, had more meaning than I realized at the time. The first thing was a lot of urinating all over his room. He had several big toys in there, and he would pee on them regularly. He'd been potty trained since he'd come home, so this was definitely behavioral.

The other thing that became obvious fairly quickly was that August was fearless. He would sneak out at night and wander the house in the pitch black. At three years old. He didn't have any fear of being in rooms alone and would sometimes fall asleep in weird places like under the guest room bed or in the living room behind the detachable sofa cushions. We'd come to check on him at night, find him missing, and that would start a search. When he wasn't in any normal place, the terror was immediate and intense. Finding him in one of those odd places, sound asleep and just as content as if he were in his own bed should have been a red flag. But we never saw it for what it was: an independent child who had no need for sleep or the comfort of the home we'd created for him.

He was also quite the hoarder. An easy chair near the TV quickly became August's spot. He would sit there and watch Sesame Street (from which he learned a considerable part of his English language!) And he would amass his collection. At one point he had an old cell phone with a cord attached to a hanger, attached to a hair brush, attached to another charger of some sort. He would walk circles around the house pretending to talk on it as he'd seen us do with the same voice inflections and all. Then all those items would come back to the chair. And they would join a silver coaster, a couple of actual toys, and whatever else he could find to gather up.

At night, he would sneak down to the kitchen and grab food. He wasn't discriminating, so it was nice that it wasn't all candy and junk food. Sometimes, it was peanut butter, sometimes granola bars. Once, thinking it was refrigerator cookie dough, he took a tube of rolled up pie dough. I found it later with one bite out of it shoved into his pillow case. I would have loved to have seen the look on his face when he bit into it and realized it had no sugar in it!

Time flies when you have two small children. Again, things were happening all along that we never connected because we didn't know what to look for. Preschool had been relatively uneventful. We knew he was smart because in less than a year, around the time of his fourth birthday we took him to a speech and hearing therapist and he was testing age appropriate in speech. He had learned enough English in ten months to be age appropriate for a four-year-old!

When it came time for kindergarten, we had to get August tested for Tuberculosis. He tested positive. That was unexpected but not shocking because Russia vaccinates for TB and it's a live virus vaccine. Still, having to get a chest X-ray to confirm that there was no presence of the virus and then nine months of isoniazid which is a powerful drug (not to mention a HUGE pill) was unsettling on top of everything else!

Starting school was exciting. He was thrilled to be able to go. He'd gone to a year of preschool without many incidents and he seemed ready. Unfortunately, in our school district, they were dealing with money woes as many communities do. One solution was to change the five-day morning and afternoon kindergarten in favor of a new system of all-day kindergarten which was every other day. It was a horrible schedule where the children went Monday, Wednesday, and every other Friday *or* Tuesday, Thursday, and every other Friday. For five-year-olds who barely know what day it is this schedule makes no sense. August went the Tuesday, Thursday and every other Friday Schedule. In October, between holidays, teacher work days, and parent/teacher conferences, August went to school only one day the entire month!

But we started off great. He was engaged, followed rules, made friends, and seemed to have a great time. We were having a conversation with his doctor about the possibility that he had ADHD due to his problems sleeping, his inability to concentrate on less active tasks other than watching TV, and other issues. We brought the questionnaire for his teacher to fill out to his conference, and, while she couldn't offer up that she agreed with us, she was more than willing to fill out the form! We were starting to paint a picture of the beginning of his issues.

We did get an ADHD diagnosis with possibly an ODD (oppositional defiant disorder) diagnosis as well. We really didn't want to put him on medication yet but we were still very worried about his lack of sleep and after speaking with his teacher, concerned that it might be affecting his abilities in school. He had qualified for ESL (English as a Second Language) services which I agreed to, though I didn't really believe he needed them. But I wanted him to get as much help as he could.

I was starting to understand how to work the school system. Realizing that ADHD qualified August for an IEP (Individualized Education Plan), he could get additional help. I was already worried about his reading ability and had bought additional materials to work with him at home. I didn't know if there was a delay due to his not being native English, the ADHD, or some other learning issue that we hadn't yet determined. We relinquished and made the decision to use medication to help August focus and keep calm during the school day.

I was getting push back from the school. We kept getting delays in their willingness to test him and begin offering him services. I knew that regardless of the results of the testing that he would qualify for services because of the ADHD. Because I knew this, I wanted him to get tested and get whatever assistance the evaluations revealed might be helpful. But I couldn't get it to happen. It seemed like they didn't agree he needed it. At the end of first grade, the decision was made to have him tested at the beginning of second grade. It appeared that the rule was that he needed to be two grade levels behind before he could get help! I was furious!

The boys' father had a sabbatical from work the summer after that first-grade year, and we had planned to start the process of moving back East. All our extended family was back there, and we wanted the boys to know their grandparents, aunts, uncles, and cousins. And we wanted to make the move before the boys got too far into school.

As August started second grade, I continued my crusade to get him an IEP. It didn't seem like I was going to be successful before we moved. But I'd hoped I could get it done in Oregon and have it in place before we moved. That didn't seem likely. I kept pressing anyway. The medication was helping but there were more and more signs that school was hard for him. One day, when I went to pick him up, the teacher was holding his hand and walking him out. He'd apparently had a particularly rough day. I went home and found his ADHD pill on the floor under his chair. We were also trying bacon in the morning to help with brain function.

He'd made a friend at school whose family was Mormon (a large percentage of our neighborhood was). They got along fairly well, but I started to see the manipulation that would become a hallmark of August's behavior start to emerge. He'd convince that boy to give him money and toys and probably more things I never learned about. His mother was very polite about it, but I was shocked. And more than a little concerned. His motivation wasn't clear to me and I was having a hard time understanding why he was doing these things. This was just the beginning of feeling this way.

He was also starting to be very good at antagonizing his brother. And his brother was getting close to being the same size he was. His dad and I joked about the day that his brother figures that out and starts to fight back. We decided he got one free swing at August and then we'd pull them apart. August could be pretty manipulative and kind of vicious to him too and his brother just seemed to take it.

While we had made the decision to start August on medication, the process is not an exact science. We started on methylphenidate, also known as Ritalin, which he took to handle the symptoms of ADHD. He also took Concerta which is a longer lasting version of the same medication. We also added Guanfacine, which is a blood pressure medicine. We used that to help him sleep. It isn't a sleeping pill but it slowly lowered his blood pressure just enough to help him drift off naturally. We tried switching from Concerta to Adderall in fall of his second-grade year. It was a disaster. One of the issues with ADHD meds is something called rebound. When the medicine leaves the system, the symptoms can be worse than when there was no medication at all. That was August on Adderall. When the medicine left his system, he was an ADHD kid times 100. It was rough. We had hoped maybe the Adderall would last a little longer, but we quickly went back to the Concerta.

On top of everything else, somehow August contracted Mononucleosis. Still scratching my head on how that one happened. But one of the things that has to happen with mono is constant blood draws to determine if the virus has passed. However, because of the fact that August was removed from the only home he'd ever known and put in a hospital full of strangers due to having pneumonia, he had some PTSD where doctors and needles were concerned. So, when it took four adults to hold him down for the first blood draw due to his extreme panic, raging, and fear, we had a conversation with the psychiatrist. He said there was no reason for him to go through that trauma. Enter the new drug: Chloral Hydrate. If you've ever heard the phrase, "being slipped a mickey," that's what Chloral Hydrate is. As for dosage, the doctor said, "Give him a teaspoon, wait a half-hour, ask him how he feels about getting his blood drawn, if he freaks out, give him more."

When it came time for the next blood draw, I tried it. He got a dose before we left the house for the 20-minute ride to the hospital. As we got closer, he seemed perfectly fine. He didn't seem to be experiencing any effects from the medicine at all. I drove around a bit to see if he'd start to get woozy. Nothing. I stopped and gave him another dose. We drove some more, maybe 15 more minutes. Then I got the magic words from

August, "When are we going to get there?" I made the quickest turn around and headed straight for the hospital. It never dawned on me what to do if he fell totally asleep because he was way too big to carry but luckily that didn't happen. He handled the blood draw just fine.

I remember at the time thinking it was maybe nice that we were using this because it might give me a hint of what he would look like if he took drugs. If you stick with me and get a few chapters down the road in this story, you'll see I had no idea what I would be seeing. This little stint was nothing.

We were able to work out a move to North Carolina that enabled August's dad to stay with his company. It was a great opportunity, since we had assumed he'd have to look for a new job for us to be able to relocate. We put the house on the market and made two trips back to Cary to look for a house. There were some hurdles, but, amazingly, we managed to close on the sale of our house in Oregon and purchase a new house in Cary in a way that let us move over spring break. This, also amazingly, was the same week for both school systems. August was able to go on vacation in Oregon and start back to school in North Carolina. I remember thinking that I knew the North Carolina schools were excellent and maybe a fresh start would allow me to get August the help I thought he needed. School was so frustrating for both of us. There had to be an easier way. Turns out, there might be, but not necessarily for me.

CHAPTER FOUR

# Elementary School

We settled into the new house very easily. It was a lovely home. I was worried about August starting at a new school. I just didn't know what to expect. It was the first time we had upset his world since we'd brought him home and I didn't know how he'd react to this huge change. But I should have known the resiliency that had gotten him this far would help him in this situation too. After spring break was over, I took him into Penny Road Elementary and his second-grade classroom. I wasn't sure how it would work coming in mid-year. The teacher was wonderfully nice. I knew there was a bus that he could take from school that dropped him off in our neighborhood, and she introduced August to a boy who took the same bus. August had always wanted to ride the bus at his old school and begged me to let him ride home. I agreed.

At the end of the day, I waited nervously at the bus stop. I wasn't sure I'd made the best decision. I met some of the neighborhood moms. The bus finally came. Off came August who immediately asked me if he could go to the house of the boy who'd helped him navigate the bus system that afternoon. Well, that was quick! I was pleased he'd made a friend so quickly. I shouldn't have worried. August was so charming and outgoing.

I was finally able to get him an IEP when we moved to North Carolina. He no longer qualified for ESL services, which was fine, but I knew he was delayed in his reading and other language areas. His spelling was horrible. And we got an occupational therapy review which got him services for increasing his fine motor skills. I was thrilled. It seemed like everything was finally on track for August to be able to start learning and get on grade level, and he was at a school where they were responding to his specific needs. Then second grade was over.

Summers can be a wonderful time when you're a kid in school. No homework, nothing to worry about, not a care in the world. There's always some hope as parents that we can weave in a little learning in the mix, but you know how it goes. This summer was a good one for August. He had a good new friend just down the street. Our neighborhood had a pool, and he loved the water.

We traveled to Indiana to see my grandmother, which the boys and I did for a week each summer to help her get ready for the annual family reunion every Independence Day weekend. My grandmother doesn't play favorites, but she loved August so much. And after he stopped letting anyone call him by his nickname, "Goose," he still let her. He was so sweet with her. He loved being at her farm where there was six acres to run free, build fires, and just be a boy. If it weren't for the mosquitos, bees, and poison ivy to which August was particularly sensitive, it would have been perfect. But, unfortunately, summers eventually come to an end.

The other special thing that happened that summer was that my sister Rachel came to live with us. She wasn't happy in Ohio and wanted a change of scenery. The boys were her only nephews and it would be a nice thing to have her close. Little did we know how much it would help to have another grown-up in the house!

If you've had a child move through elementary school you know that the jump from second to third grade is the greatest one in all of the elementary grades. The increase in expectation of executive function is huge. The knowledge base is larger and it seems like they go from being hand-held and spoon-fed all the time to having a much greater requirement of performance.

The first thing about third grade was that personality-wise, his teacher was the complete opposite from his second-grade teacher. This is how I came to realize during August's third grade year the importance of the teacher match to his success. In fact, a lot of *my* education about August's education came from this year. I'm sure her style might work for some children, but for kids like August, it was a recipe for disaster.

As we moved into that third-grade year, August's behavior got more and more aggressive and agitated. We had moved in the Spring and I was still searching for a good match in a new therapist. We had been going to one who thought that August might have Asperger's. I knew in my heart that wasn't the case. He was much too social and much too engaged. We were relying on his pediatrician, a nurse practitioner whom I adored, to manage his medication.

At school, we were having continuing and escalating problems. His relationship with his teacher was in a decline, due partly to her behavior and partly to his. His school work wasn't going well and homework was a battle as well. We continued to have episodes of food hoarding, lack of sleeping at night, stealing, and other problematic behaviors. I was volunteering at school in the library so I could have a chance to keep an eye on what was happening with August. He knew he was having trouble in school, so he starting finding short cuts to keep an image he wanted to project. If he couldn't get the answers on a test right, the best thing he could do to make himself look good was to finish first. He'd carry around the biggest, thickest book he could and would take reading tests on these books, even though he hadn't read even one page. These manipulation behaviors started a pattern, which I saw throughout the Fall. It was like he developed a boldness that hadn't existed before.

He also started to steal from his grandparents. His grandfather collected tubes of state quarters and small pocket knives among other things. This was particularly embarrassing to his father. It drove me crazy because I wanted him to defend his son whom I knew had something going on, but since I didn't know what was really wrong, I had no explanation to give. The frustration was mounting for all of us.

After Christmas, things got even worse. His behavior went way off the rails with anger and problems at school that became constant. In mid-January, we sat down with his teacher to discuss the situation. It was a tense meeting because I wasn't happy with how she was running her classroom, and I knew it was an ineffective environment for August. She let us know that his behavior was problematic. I talked about how after holidays August has always had a hard time settling back in. She didn't seem to consider that a valid explanation. She asked about our plans for next year and questioned if we'd ever considered homeschooling. We had in fact been looking at other schools. Our school system was a model for the country in having a magnet program that allowed for schools with a host of different curricula and we were exploring others that might be a better fit for August. We said we were looking at possibly moving August next year. We did say that we were looking at a variety of options for next year. And our son's teacher, the woman in whom we were placing our confidence and who we hoped was loving and caring for our 8-year-old son said, "You don't have to wait until next year."

My heart dropped. I was speechless. Every fiber of my mama bear anger welled up and it took all I had not to march straight to the principal's office. No wonder August was so anxious and feeling so oppositional to his teacher.

I determined at that moment that we were going to have to survive this year with this teacher who obviously wasn't interested at all in working with August or understanding him. And while I didn't fully understand him myself, I knew he had more than just a learning issue, and I needed help to understand what was going on.

He continued to get into trouble at school and his teacher continued to be a problem rather than a solution. I did end up talking with the principal, which was a waste of time. His behavior was getting more and more aggressive and outrageous, until one Wednesday...

I don't remember the date. Just the day. I don't really know why, maybe self-preservation. It was early Spring and we'd been in chaos mode for a while doing battle to get homework done and dealing with school behavior problems. I don't really know what happened that made this day so different. But after school, things went horribly wrong.

We had a routine. He got a 4-hour Ritalin boost after school because his 12-hour medication never lasted 12 hours. Then we got a snack and jumped into homework. It never worked if we tried to put off homework because the combination of his getting tired and being off medication later in the evening made it impossible.

That Wednesday he came home and we started to do what we normally do. But he was having none of it. He was immediately aggressive and angry and argumentative. I'd become accustomed to this by now and had a few tricks to get him back on track, but this escalated so fast I wasn't prepared for what happened next. The rage grew and became so intense he was like someone I didn't know. I sent him to his room, which I later learned was a mistake but at the time I just needed to separate us. Homework was obviously not going to happen. This was the beginning of three hours of battle. He was screaming and I was screaming. Everything in his room became a projectile and a weapon. Every time I went into the room, something was hurled in my direction. Along with screaming threats and more anger than I thought a little body could hold. He was like a wild animal. At the least, he was someone I hardly knew. To protect myself, I had to first remove all the knobs off his dresser. Then it was all the toys. Then it was all the hangers, clothing, and shoes in the closet. I was terrified. His brother was in the house and I didn't know what to do. I kept him downstairs, and I think he was fine but I wasn't sure. I called his dad at work and told him that something very wrong was happening.

This went on for hours. I had to hold the door closed to protect myself and my younger son. When I went in to see if I could reason with him, August had found something else to throw. When the raging finally stopped, his room had a bed and a dresser with no knobs. Everything else had been taken out. Everything an 8-year-old could lift was gone. Books and hats and games and pictures and even some of the clothes in his dresser.

I was spent. It was like having battle fatigue. I was raw and confused and so sad. My beautiful boy whom I knew was troubled had just had some sort of mental breakdown that I couldn't help him through. I was devastated. Later that night, his father and I discussed what to do next. We knew we were dealing with something much more serious than ADHD or anything we could handle. It had been escalating for a while and the dam seemed to have broken.

We made the decision to keep him home from school the next day and take him to the doctor. Our wonderful nurse practitioner agreed to see us in the morning. When we went in, I explained what had been happening, and then the events of the previous night. She agreed that he had experienced some sort of mental break and wanted to discuss things with a psychiatrist colleague. After a bit she came back in. She said they discussed the option of whether or not to admit him but that based on the fact that he was calm at the moment decided not to. She said she wanted to get us in to see the psychiatrist as soon as possible, but he had no immediate openings. But the other psychiatrist in his office had an opening next Tuesday. We agreed to the appointment. Our NP also put him on a very strong antipsychotic called Seroquel. The dosage was to basically give it to him until he passes out.

A while after it happened, I was with a friend and mentioned that August was taking Seroquel. She mentioned that she had taken it for her bipolar disorder. She was surprised August took such a powerful drug. She said she quartered them and then could lick the quarter pill and feel the effects. I said, "August takes four." That's where we were when we walked into the psychiatrist's office the following Tuesday.

After all the psychiatrists we'd seen and all the medications August had been on, I was naturally skeptical when we walked into the psychiatrist's office. Plus, I hadn't researched him. While I trusted August's NP tremendously, I was desperate and going on her recommendation that this was the guy we needed at this moment. We had a lot of history to catch him up on but it didn't take him long to assess the situation. Particularly when we got to the more recent behaviors of hoarding, raging, stealing, and manipulation. He kept him on the Seroquel and we set a meeting for the next week.

I was knowledgeable about the basics of "freeze, fight,

or flight." I knew how people respond when faced with a traumatic or stressful situation with the choices of freezing, fighting, or running away. I was now in that space 24/7. My whole world had turned upside down in a week. I never knew what the next minute would bring and I was constantly on alert. Sending him to school was terrifying; his walking back in the door at the end of the day was terrifying. Asking him to do homework was terrifying. In many ways, my own son had become a stranger to me and I didn't know what to expect from moment to moment. The medication was helpful, but we couldn't keep him drugged all the time.

His behaviors did continue to change. The raging continued and he seemed to want to do anything he could think of that would push the last unpushed button. He worked diligently on punching and digging a hole from his bedroom out into the hallway for no reason other than just the destructiveness of the effort. He wasn't successful, thank goodness, but it required a major repair job.

Swearing was an impressive addition, one that we didn't handle at all well. I'm not sure why. I think because it seemed very personal for some reason. In the middle of the most violent of rages, August would just start saying whatever swear word he could think of. Not even in context. He'd just blurt out "shit" or "hell" or "damn" in rapid succession. He'd heard them I'm sure on the bus or in school as we were very careful not to use them at home (at least not around the boys!) It was almost humorous at times to hear him just say, "Shit, shit, shit, shit..." over and over again. He seemed to feel like he was getting away with something. He'd have a smile on his face. I did something I never thought I'd ever do; I put a small piece of soap in his mouth for just a second to make him stop. This was how desperate I felt. That was how out of control we both were. We all were. All of us were going crazy.

When I told the psychiatrist, he was quick to tell me that wasn't something that was done anymore. I knew that and I felt horrible about it. But when you have a totally out-of-control child, you become an out-of-control parent. You just want it to stop. After hours and hours of the raging and screaming and physical thrashing, you're exhausted and definitely not thinking clearly. I certainly wasn't. And part of me knew I was most likely doing more harm than good. But it just needed to stop.

When we met again with the psychiatrist, we talked further about what had been happening at home and at school. We discussed more his history before the adoption as much as we knew. The picture we drew out became clear for him and the psychiatrist said the words no other psychiatrist had ever said before. That our son was suffering from Reactive Attachment Disorder.

## CHAPTER FIVE

# The Diagnosis

want to begin with explaining the clinical definition of Reactive Attachment Disorder. It helps to get a basis for what we are dealing with. *The Diagnostic and Statistical Manual 5th Edition (DSM-5)* is the definitive source for how mental illnesses are described and identified. This book is used by all clinicians and medical personnel to understand the variety of mental disorders.

RAD wasn't identified until the third edition even though the implications of early childhood neglect have been studied for years. And even with that, so much is still unknown about the factors of maternal neglect, early child abuse, and failure to thrive that will affect a child long after infancy.

When we'd been going through classes to consider foster care adoption, I remember seeing one overly xeroxed article on Attachment Disorder. One. But that's it. Nothing in any of the classes themselves or any of the international adoption literature talked about Attachment Disorder. And certainly not its evil twin Reactive Attachment Disorder. So, I'd heard of it. sort of. But that was it. It was clearly not at all on my radar of what could possibly be going on with my son and causing these scary, drastic behaviors. And because of that, I had no clue where to start to comprehend what we were dealing with and understand what was going on in my son.

His new psychiatrist was excellent at explaining what happens to children who develop RAD. And let me digress a bit by saying there are a lot of kid's t-shirts out in the world that say, "I'm a RAD kid" referencing the retro 60s slang for being cool or great. Boy is that a weird oxymoron. And let me digress a little further by saying I've included the *DSM-5* description at the end of the book so you can understand in an objective way what exactly reactive attachment disorder is. And later on, I'll talk a little about what the prevailing theory is about RAD to date.

But when he revealed this diagnosis, the psychiatrist

explained it as all children need to bond with a primary caregiver when they're infants. Usually, that's the mother due to nursing, but it can be any person who is responsible for their basic needs. When they cry, the infant is fed, changed, picked up, and soothed, so they learn that they can rely on that primary caregiver. They learn trust because every time they cry, their needs are met. Over and over and over again. Now for children who are abused or neglected in those first 1,000 days, those first three years of life, that doesn't happen. The care is sporadic or even nonexistent. When they cry, the response may come from a variety of people or not at all. The response may not be a fulfillment of needs or worse, some negative treatment. The child learns that the adults in their life cannot be relied on. They learn not to trust them, and, subsequently, they learn not to trust anyone.

And this isn't just a learned behavior. It's a physiological change that happens in the child's brain. As a child develops the ability to trust while consistent needs are being met, synapses in the brain are formed that allow the brain to understand the concept of trust and be able to transfer it to other people and situations. If there's no primary caregiver providing consistent care, then those synapses are pruned and they have no understanding of trust or ability to trust other people in any other situations.

This results in a child who is intently fixated on controlling all situations because they don't believe they can depend on anyone else for even their most basic needs. They're also extremely impulsive because they're in a constant state of heightened alert due to not ever knowing who they can rely on and where their resources may come from. They take what they can get and do what they can do whenever the situation presents itself. They have an amazing ability to manipulate people and situations because of the need to control. The lack of trust means that people, things, and situations are only tools to get what they need and nothing of value or attachment.

I'll get into the various treatment modalities in later chapters, but one of the most, if not the most, well-known writers and educators on the subject of RAD is Nancy Thomas. Soon after August was diagnosed, I dove into anything and everything I could get my hands on and this was one of the first things I read:

THE FROZEN LAKE by Nancy L. Thomas

"In order to understand what an unattached child feels like, one must understand his perspective. Imagine that you are the young child who must cross a frozen lake in the autumn to reach your home. As you are walking across the lake alone, you fall suddenly and unexpectedly through the ice. Shocked and cold in the dark, you can't even cry for help. You struggle for your very life; you struggle to the surface. Locating the jagged opening, you drag yourself through the air and crawl back into the woods from where you started. You decide to live there and never, never to return onto the ice. As weeks go by you see others on the lake ice skating and crossing the ice. If you go onto it, you will die.

Your family across the pond hears the sad news that the temperature will drop to sub-zero this night. So, a brave and caring family member (that is you, the parent!) searches and finds you to bring you home to love and warmth. The family member attempts to help you cross the ice by supporting and encouraging, pulling and prodding. You, believing you will die, fight for your life by kicking, screaming, punching and yelling (even obscenities) to get the other person away from you. Every effort is spent in attempting to disengage from this family member. The family member fights for your life, knowing you must have the love and warmth of home for your very survival. They take the blows you dish out and continue to pull you across the ice to home, knowing it's your only chance.

The ice represents the strength of the bond and your ability to trust. It was damaged by the break in your connection to someone you trusted. Some children have numerous bonding breaks throughout their young lives. This is like crashing them into the ice water each time they are moved, scarring and chilling their hearts against ever loving and bonding again."

This story is such a stark understanding of what's happening in the minds of these traumatized children, and more importantly, in the mind of my sweet August. And I couldn't see how it could possibly get better.

Further conversations with the psychiatrist were about what his ideas of treatment and prognosis looked like. His theory was that it took three years of treatment and healing for every one year of trauma. That's fine if we only count the three years before the adoption. That would be nine years, he could be healed by the time he was 18. But he was already nine now and we seemed far from well. Part of that stemmed from not knowing what we were doing and parenting him completely wrong for the last six years because we had therapists who didn't know what RAD was and we weren't informed enough to ask the right questions. So, I added those years as well. Nine years times three. Awesome. He'll be all better by the time he's 27.

Well, we better get started.

The first part was finding medication that would work. The raging, anxiety, and other defiant behaviors needed to be addressed. My concern was that as long as August was so out of control, we were never going to be able to make any progress on healing. We needed to get him to a place where we could actually reach him. The psychiatrist's first suggestion was Zoloft. It's a pretty common anti-anxiety, anti-depression medication. So, we started with that. We also made Focalin his ADHD medication. Focalin is a long-acting medication (12-hour is what it says on the packaging) and it allows taking smaller (less than half) doses of other types of ADHD meds. It didn't last 12 hours for August, and we had to give him a Ritalin supplement when he got home but it worked the best of anything we'd tried until that point.

So, we now had our diagnosis and our new medication. And I had my marching orders. Time to learn everything ever written about reactive attachment disorder. I didn't know anything about it. I didn't know how to parent a child with it, of course, since I didn't know what it was. And I was convinced what I'd done to date had been horribly wrong. But what I found was that none of the "experts" out in the world seemed to know what to tell parents to do either. Oh great.

When I googled reactive attachment disorder, back in 2007, there was very little to find. The one thing that I remember was www.radkid.com (I think). It doesn't exist anymore. It gave a list of attributes of children with RAD. And it gave a description of the behaviors of adults with RAD. And let's just say none of them were flattering. And then there was the list of people the author of this website believed probably had RAD. And it wasn't a list you want to be on. Some celebrated bad guys like Jeffrey Dahmer, Adolph Hitler, and others. My jaw dropped. I couldn't believe what I was reading. I was still really new to all of this and still learning what it meant. But a website that's lumping my child in with these maniacs? I was rocked to my core. This wasn't what I signed up for.

Further googling got me to Nancy Thomas. It seemed all roads were leading to her and her book, *When Love Is Not*

*Enough.* I got it as soon as I could. I also picked up *Beyond Consequences, Logic and Control: A Love-Based Approach to Helping Attachment-Challenged Children with Severe Behaviors* by Heather Forbes and Bryan T. Post. I was so hungry for information I inhaled both the books. And I was amazed by the almost total opposite approach the two books took on how to deal with children with RAD. **The reviews that follow are my opinions of what these books recommend. Many parents of RAD children I've talked with over the years have found success with the advice from these authors. They just weren't for me.

Nancy Thomas warns that children with RAD may never have a capacity for loving their adoptive parents (or biological parents if the RAD is due to some early childhood trauma in the family). The answer is to gain obedience. To make the child understand who is in charge (the parents) and that the child doesn't have any ability to control or manipulate the situation. The recommendations of consequences were severe and made sure that the child knew the parents were running the show. It just didn't seem like the kind of relationship I wanted with August.

The second book seemed to be written as a response to Nancy Thomas. It described several of the typical RAD behaviors then how to take a more loving, empathetic approach to dealing with them. While I completely agreed that coming from a place of anger and fear isn't setting yourself up for success as a parent dealing with a RAD child, I couldn't get beside their methods of empathy either. There just didn't seem to be enough consequences for the child's behaviors. I didn't see how the child was going to understand how to change and heal from this method.

I ended up not using methods suggested by either of these books partly because I was busy for a few weeks dealing with August on Zoloft. One of the other issues the psychiatrist mentioned was that he could ALSO (like we didn't have enough to process) be bi-polar. When we started him on the Zoloft the psychiatrist warned that people who are bi-polar can have adverse reactions to Zoloft. But he didn't really specify what that might be. Didn't take long to figure that out. Relieving depression and anxiety turned into making August think he was made of titanium. He was climbing trees, like to the super-scary tops of trees. He set fires in the front yard. Not big fires, but even small fires aren't something you want your 9-year-old doing unsupervised. One time, I came into his room to find him hanging out his second-story window. Stuff like that were the adverse reactions. Remember that time on the airplane from Moscow when the Benadryl didn't work? Yep. That's something people with bi-polar disorder tend to have too. They get the excitability side, not the drowsiness. However, it's hard to diagnose bi-polar in children, so the psychiatrist was hesitant to say for sure. But it was looking likely.

We obviously moved off the Zoloft and onto Risperdal. This is another pretty common anti-anxiety drug. We started to notice some changes. He seemed to get calmer for a while when the drug was in its full effect. It didn't last as long as it was supposed to and wore off before he got home from school, but we were getting through school. We might survive third grade after all. I was hopeful that we might be getting to a point where we could start some healing, that the worst was behind us. I was still quite naïve.

We did make it through third grade. One memory I have that has stayed with me of that year was sitting in the library one morning when the lockdown drill alarm rang. I volunteered there because it got me in the school and by third grade there weren't room parents anymore. I remember being hunkered down in the A/V room in the dark with the librarian and another parent. August's class was out in a trailer due to incessant overcrowding in the fast-growing Raleigh/

Durham/Cary school system. Completely exposed to anyone who might wander onto the campus grounds. As frustrating as the year had been, as much anxiety as the situation with August had created, and as many tears as I had shed, the only thought I had was that if this were a real active shooter situation, no one could have stopped me from getting to that trailer to my child.

## CHAPTER SIX

# My child Has RAD, Now What?

We had a diagnosis and we'd finally found a medication cocktail that seemed to be working. We had found Focalin to be our ADHD medicine and that with the Risperdal plus an extra little hit of 4-hour Ritalin when he got home from school (we never found a 12-hour medication that LASTED 12 hours!) got us to a place where August was calm enough to pay attention and interact with. I wasn't a fan of all the medications, resisted adding new ones. But what I finally had to realize was that the medication got August to a place where he was reachable. And that meant mentally for teaching him and emotionally for bonding with him. Unmedicated, August didn't want or need anything or anyone. His goals were very primitive: food and stimulation. But he would interact on a higher level with more thought if he were medicated. So, the medication was an integral part of the process.

Obviously, our experience with third grade wasn't good. I was afraid he was "marked" at that school due to all the problems he'd had and the way his teacher had handled things. And his brother was heading into kindergarten so it was a good time to consider moving schools if we were going to do it. One of the additional reasons for the move from Portland was the excellent school system in the Raleigh/Cary area. Wake County, many years earlier, had started a magnet school system to attract students from the suburbs into the inner-city schools. Essentially, it integrated the schools without forced bussing. The schools in the downtown areas have specialized curriculum that are very attractive.

After touring several, we decided on Conn Elementary, which had a curriculum called "Active Learning and Technology." They had a close-circuit TV studio that broadcasted a morning news show, smartboards in most of the classrooms, 200 speakers brought in the previous year, field trips for each grade three to four times a year. There were many wonderful aspects for both boys.

What I didn't have the ability to impact was the teacher match. As I had found out with third grade, it's huge for August. But at a new school, I had no knowledge of the teachers or their personalities. However, armed with my new knowledge and understanding of August's issues, I felt like I could make my case and change his teacher if it seemed like it needed to happen early on.

We walked in on the first day, and it was like we'd won the teacher lottery. There, in yet another trailer, unfortunately, stood a bald, muscular African-American man. He had a goatee beard and a bow tie. And he was awesome. It may seem strange that I describe him in such detail but it's important to know how just the initial look of him was appealing to August. He looked tough and cool, had a deep voice, and talked with slang. He couldn't have been more opposite the uptight, tense, cranky third-grade teacher we'd just endured.

Couple this with a principal I fell in love with by the end of the first week. She learned the names of each of the several hundred students in her care within days. She was present everywhere. I had decided to volunteer in my younger son's kindergarten class (they didn't allow parents in the upper grades, so this was mostly—like the library—to get me in the building with August). I was there every week for an afternoon helping with reading or sorting papers or helping with whatever needed doing. There was a teacher's aide in the room also, but in the magnet schools, the disparity of skills and abilities among the children was stark. This population included homeless children and children in homes with no books or parents who could help with homework. I watched the teacher's aide in my younger son's room give children toothbrushes and clean socks. Because of this school's demographics, the principal and the entire counseling and administrative team was well-versed in dealing with children with traumatic home lives. This gave them a much better level of understanding than the more homogenous suburban school we were coming from.

We launched into the school year and I was—dare I say it—hopeful that we might have found a place where August could thrive. The first chance to see if I was right came in October when I had a meeting with his entire IEP team. This included his primary teacher, the IEP teacher, the counselor, and a host of other folks I can't even remember. This was one of the most delightful IEP meetings I've ever had. Possibly the only one. Because there they all were, reading August's file from his previous school with confused looks on their faces. And then someone was bold enough to ask what had happened at the prior school. Because the August they were seeing now looked nothing like the one described in the write-ups from his previous teachers and administrators.

I did my best not to shout "Hallelujah!" But it confirmed right away that our decision to move him had been right. Obviously, August wasn't behaving badly and was doing his work the way he needed to. I was thrilled! But the only way to keep this up was to make sure he had the accommodations he needed to be successful. And luckily the school was willing to do what he needed. In addition to all the regular things that were put into place for students with ADHD and his learning issues, we arranged for him to be able to leave the classroom if his anxiety was getting too overwhelming. He could sign out like he was going to the bathroom and run around the track which was right outside the trailer where his classroom was. He also tended to get into more trouble when there was a substitute because the whole class was more disruptive. On those days, he was allowed to remove himself and go to the office so he didn't get into trouble. To continue to work on the issue of his fine motor skills problems he was allowed to work directly at the computer instead of writing out papers long-hand, which was so frustrating for him.

The school's willingness to work with August and remove barriers that made him anxious and frustrated was such a welcome change from the prior school experience. I thought we were really heading in the right direction now and it would be smooth sailing from now on. I had relaxed a little too soon.

Because while things were definitely going much better at school, at home, it was a different story. Every day, I would pick the boys up from the bus stop and drive them home. Took about 10 minutes. As we pulled into the driveway, I would open the garage door and see if I could time it so that I could get the car into the garage and the door down before August could bolt out of the car and run away. It meant a lot of the time racing into the garage at an unsafe speed or with the door barely clearing the ceiling of the car. Because August knew that as soon as we hit the house, it would be time for homework, and he didn't want any part of that. This didn't happen every day, but if he knew he had something he didn't want to do, his behavior let me know pretty quick.

I would wait inside and he would eventually show up on the back porch. If I made any motion to open the door, he'd take off again. How long this would last would depend on how hungry and tired he was. On one occasion, my sister and I did go after him. We chased him down the street and pulled him out from under the deck of a neighbor's house. We wrangled him into the car and got him to the emergency room. This particular battle had gone on for a while when we finally caught him and I wasn't sure we'd be able to calm him back down. I called the psychiatrist and we discussed whether it was time to hospitalize him. Then I found out that in our town the law is that anyone who is transferred to a psychiatric facility has to go in handcuffs. The idea of having my little boy go out in handcuffs was just heartbreaking to me. As you read on, you'll see I got over this, but I couldn't make that decision that day. So, we took him home. It remained one of those decisions that I wonder if I'd made a difference choice would things down the road have gone differently. I don't think it's possible for children with RAD to be "scared straight." I don't believe there can be that one overwhelming event that hits them between the eyes and makes them see the error of their thinking. RAD doesn't work like that. For one, it's not just psychological; it's also physiological, and the brain doesn't grow overnight. And while we can believe in love at first sight or see someone and just know we're not going to like them; trust can only be developed over time. And that's the one thing RAD kiddos just don't have the ability to feel.

The rages that started our path to RAD weren't a daily occurrence but often enough. We had adopted what the psychiatrist had termed, "hold him till he likes it" therapy. It consisted of sitting with August on the floor with his back to me and in between my legs. I'd wrap my legs around his, then one of my arms around both of his. The other arm was used to hold his head so that he wouldn't head-butt me. He'd struggle and we'd stay like this until he'd calm down. I'd talk to him, tell him jokes, try and get him to relax. Sometimes, it could take an hour. Occasionally, it took longer. Hopefully, if I was able, I'd get him in his room or at least get him into a room where I could close the door. Once, that didn't happen and his brother walked by. I casually said, "Everything's fine!" while struggling to keep August held in place. His brother just said, "It doesn't look fine," and kept on walking. The pain of the potential damage done to one child while trying to heal the other wasn't lost on me.

At the end of the school year, I sat down with the principal and almost begged for her to consider letting his teacher move with him to fifth grade. It had been such an ideal match, the thought of starting over was daunting. I explained how much better this had been than third grade and what I had learned about the importance of that relationship for August. She had apparently seen that for other students as well, for, in the fall, the entire fourth grade team had looped up to fifth grade, and August had the same teacher! I'm not sure who was happier, me or August! Maybe we could have a year with a bit of a breather.

Fifth grade did go fairly uneventfully, considering the bar is a little higher for RAD kiddos, but we didn't escape without more than our share of drama. August got his first suspension for bringing a pocket knife to school and got into his first fight. We were still having a time getting him to do any homework without a major battle. This was being further exacerbated by the fact that his brother, now in first grade was winning state writing contests and proving to be an excellent student. Of course, we didn't make any comparisons, but August knew. And his lack of caring about school grew.

As we rounded out elementary school it was time to start considering the best options for middle school. As with being able to change his elementary school, we were blessed with options to consider based on both curriculum and schedule. There were both traditional and year-round calendar schools in our area. We knew that a year-round schedule might be a good option for August as it would give him less of a big gap of down time for loss of information. But it didn't match up at all with his brother's traditional schedule. So, we found a middle school that had a modified year-round calendar that shortened the summer break but put larger breaks in between quarters. We decided this seemed like a good compromise. It would give August some good break periods but still align with his brother's calendar enough. And the curriculum was through one of the local universities so there would again be a lot of hands-on learning. Once again, our best-laid plans and intentions weren't enough to combat what reactive attachment disorder was about to throw at us. Not by a long shot.

CHAPTER SEVEN

# Middle School

As a general disclaimer, I want to protest that schools start earlier and earlier as grades go up. Small children get up super early. Older children can sleep till noon. This is completely backwards. And the fact that no one has realized this and adjusted school start times accordingly is ridiculous. I just want to be on record here.

I say this because August had to be at the bus stop at 6:20 every morning. And that was to get on the first of two buses he had to ride. That bus took him to one of the high schools where he then got on another bus that took him to school. Between the ADHD and the impulsivity August isn't always too aware of his surroundings so the fact that he made it to the correct school every day was amazing to me.

The teachers at his middle school were set up in teaching teams so that there were two teachers per team. One taught English and social studies and one taught math and science. August's strongest subjects were always math and science. His struggles had always been in language arts, particularly reading, and I was convinced he had some sort of learning issue but nothing had ever been diagnosed. This would be the year all that got turned on its head. Because, as I have mentioned and will continue to drive home, it's all about the teacher match.

My expectation was that middle school would be no different from what we'd experienced in elementary school. Struggles with grammar and spelling. Huge pushback with reading. And relatively little problems with math and science by comparison. From day one it was the exact opposite. August put up much less fight regarding homework in English and social studies. We got no behavior reports from that teacher. But the anxiety levels were through the roof when it came to math and science. The behavior issues were nearly constant in those classes.

We suffered through the Fall but it was obvious things were only getting worse. Add to the math and science class problems, August hated his bus driver. I don't know why, maybe it was the hour of the day. But there was ongoing talk about how much he didn't like her. August didn't seem to be learning anything and his behavior was spiraling out of control. I talked to the psychiatrist and asked him if he would participate in a call with the teachers and dean to try and come up with a plan. I needed the psychiatrist to help explain to them, better than I could, how August thinks, so they could understand some of the requests I needed to make.

We got the meeting with the psychiatrist on the phone. He went through very clearly how children with reactive attachment disorder have trust and control issues. He explained that adults in August's life get put into two distinct groups: those he trusts (likes) and those he doesn't trust (dislikes). And it's very hard, pretty much impossible, to get out of that "doesn't trust" group once you're in it. We discussed how the science and math teacher and the bus driver had gotten themselves in that group. I explained how unusual it was for August to be doing so much better in English and social studies and how that's further evidence of the importance of the teacher relationship. We talked about whether the teacher team could be changed so that August could get a different math and science teacher. Unfortunately, we were told we couldn't break up the teams and if he got a new math and science teacher, he'd lost the English and social studies teacher whom he loved. Ack! They were missing the issue here...

However, as August is so good at doing, he fixed the problem for us. By creating an even bigger one. Like most kids his age, the lure of electronics was huge. August wanted a cell phone so bad it consumed him. He'd been very materialistic for some time, being fascinated by name-brand clothing and shoes, but the cell phone was the holy grail. Early in the second half of the year, I got a call from the school that a girl was missing a cell phone. The school resource officer was investigating. They'd questioned August about whether he knew anything about it. He had, of course, denied any knowledge. But then the girl's mom produced the $200 phone bill including a call to August's best friend who lived right down the street from our house. And didn't go to the same school. Which made it very hard to pin it on anyone else.

As soon as August started getting questioned, he'd gotten rid of the phone. But he was still guilty of taking it and there was still the matter of the bill he'd racked up. We are now about to have our first experience with the criminal justice system. Raleigh has a wonderful program for first-time teenage offenders called Teen Court. It's run for and by teens and cases are referred there that are nonviolent and not drug related. Teens who have previously been defendants serve as attorneys and jurors. They make the decisions about sentencing in conjunction with an actual judge. After the sentencing requirements have been met (restitution, community service, etc.) then the offense is expunged.

We tried our best to scare him to death about what was happening. Make sure he understood the severity of the situation. It was hard to see if he really got it. We met with the teen court "lawyer," the teenager who would serve as August's attorney and some grown-ups who talked us through the process. The "lawyer" said that he wanted me to talk about August's RAD as part of his defense. I agreed but wasn't sure what his plan was.

We got to the court date and there we were in an actual looking courtroom but everyone was a teenager except the people in the gallery who I imagine had brought the children there and the judge. Things began very formally with reading the charges, all much like a "real" trial. August's lawyer got up and talked a little about him and his having reactive attachment disorder. Then he asked me to explain what that was. I stood up and talked about early childhood trauma and neglect. I talked about its effect on the brain development. I talked about how it manifests itself in impulsivity and control issues.

When I was done, the "lawyer" basically said that August's illness was responsible for his actions. And the jury of other teenagers seem to buy that. The judge said that August got away with it because he shouldn't have been allowed to use his mental health as an excuse for his crime. I had helped August get away with a crime by explaining his reactive attachment disorder. As you read on, you'll find it wouldn't be the first time.

He was required to do community service to earn money that would serve as restitution to pay for the $200 cell phone bill he'd incurred. This required taking him downtown to an office every week for 10 weeks where he would spend four hours cleaning up city parks, planting, and doing various other jobs. He didn't like getting up early on a Saturday but I think he liked going more than he let on. He got that done and then we had to make a decision about school.

The situation with the math and science teacher wasn't improving. And it was infecting everything that was going well. It didn't seem like we were going to be able to save this school year. In consultation with the psychiatrist, we decided to take him out of public school and begin to homeschool him. The thought was that not only could he get some control over his education, which he might respond well to, but he and I would have some quality time together that might help with bonding. In the late winter of sixth grade, we withdrew August from school and he and I began the homeschool adventure.

CHAPTER EIGHT

## Homeschool

Homeschooling is not for the faint of heart. It isn't all walking hand in hand with your child through museums. It isn't hiking along creeks looking at leaves and bugs. It isn't exciting chemistry experiments in your kitchen at home. And there are a lot of other things it isn't when you're homeschooling a child with reactive attachment disorder.

I looked forward to what I hoped it would be. A chance to spend some intentional, quality time with August. A chance for him to learn in an environment where he'd have some control and maybe be able to thrive with less distractions. The opportunity for him to maybe do some healing, since we wouldn't have so much school pressure to deal with adding to the anxiety.

I purchased a system called K-12. It came with all the teacher resources, workbooks and online resources for all the core classes—math, English, history/social studies, science. The big boxes came with lots of wonderful tools and gadgets including a microscope. Fortunately, my poor housecleaning skills allowed for some dead flies for August to look at under the microscope right away! Seemed like we were ready to go.

I had to get his brother off to school every morning so I let August have an easier morning. He helped me do the dishes and get the kitchen cleaned up, then we went upstairs to the office where "school" happened. One of the things he liked about the idea of homeschool was how much less time it was going to take. Frankly, that didn't bother me either! It's amazing how much of the school day is wasted with just moving around! I gave him control over the order we did subjects. He seemed to like the ability to pick what order we did things. Some subjects happened with old-fashioned paper and pencil; some happened with online worksheets, tests, and other materials.

It was interesting that he immediately reverted back to liking his favorite subjects pre-bad teacher matches. English and social studies and history were out. Science and math were back in. Anything involving words was like pulling teeth to get him to work on. I even found history comic books! But it was still a challenge. It was so hard for him. With all the additional attention struggles he had, it broke my heart to think about how hard school must have been for him with all the challenges he dealt with. I wanted to try to make this work. I wanted it to be a successful experience for both of us.

We finished out what was the balance of his sixth-grade year. My sister had moved to Memphis to take a new job, so things were a lot quieter in the house. The boys both had plans for attending summer camps; both day camps and week-long overnight camps. August was going to go to a week-long Methodist camp down in southern North Carolina. This was a leap of faith I wasn't sure I was ready for but it seemed like something that might be good for August, so leaping we did.

Showing up at camp was an amazing experience. I'd never done a "sleep away" camp growing up. But I'd done overnight field trips and other camps to know what's involved with getting kids checked in. Camp staff have to learn what's needed to know to keep campers alive for the time they're in their care. One of the most incredible new things I experienced was the lines to turn in medications. First of all, there were two of them. There was one line just for those handing in inhalers! And a separate line for us handing over other kinds of medications. I waited patiently in the long line and couldn't help but hear that the child in front of me was dropping off a bottle of Tums. What was going on in that poor child's world that his anxiety levels were so off the charts? I handed over August's three different medications and explained their different schedules and dosages. I then turned around and didn't look back just in case they were rolling their eyes or growling at me.

August actually had a good week. He participated in everything (mostly). The phone never rang (whew!) He came home with someone else's underwear on. It was some name brand that I can't remember and I asked him why. He said another boy gave them to him. I remarked that it was nice but it's UNDERWEAR! As I unpacked his bag, I realized that his underwear was still in the corner of his bag where I'd packed it. Apparently, I should have put it in a more obvious part of the suitcase.

My sister wasn't the only one who relocated during this time. So did August's psychiatrist, the one who'd given us the RAD diagnosis. The one who was guiding us along this minefield to figure out how to navigate his behaviors and moods was moving out of town. The thought of having to find another therapist was terrifying. And I'm not overstating that. I was terrified. I didn't know if I could go through the process again of finding someone who could understand what we were going through. This doctor was the fourth one and the one who finally gave me an insight into my child. How many more therapists was I going to have to go through to find another one who got it? I was running out of time to make more mistakes. August was getting older and puberty was around the corner which would add a whole other layer of issues to deal with. I needed to keep the focus on August's healing, and I needed a partner in that process who knew what they were doing.

I began the hunt again for a new therapist. I didn't necessarily need a psychiatrist because our nurse practitioner could take care of the medications but I did need someone who could pick up where the psychiatrist left off. After some looking around, we found one who seemed to be a good fit, nowhere near convenient in location, but, for the right person, that's no big deal.

We started meeting with the new therapist and guess what? The first thing I had to do was explain what reactive attachment disorder was. The whole thing. His whole story. All the behaviors that led to the diagnosis, the conversations and progress and issues we'd worked through with the previous psychiatrist and his primary care NP. At the next visit, the therapist said he'd discussed RAD with his coworkers and none of them had heard of it and they were all really shocked and interested in it. Yeah, that's what you want to hear from your therapist. That you have presented him with a child who has a disorder that stumped him. But August liked him so we stayed. I was still homeschooling and exhausted, so we stayed.

Our area had a very active homeschooling community and we were able to join a wonderful group that had regular social activities. It was interesting because families come to homeschooling for a variety of reasons. Several of them are dietary. When we had potlucks everything that everyone brought had to be egg, dairy, nut, gluten, and sugar-free. A lot were also meat-free. The children got along very well at all these get togethers, which was great. I never had any problems with August. We also joined a smaller group that was just a history study group. We rotated to a different family's house and studied a different historical topic with crafts, games, food, and reading. Again, August did really well in this small group of very diverse children.

Homeschooling also offered us the opportunity to do a lot of other out-of-the-box activities. We studied science on nature walks. We learned about anatomy cutting up a chicken. We learned music, as I gave August piano lessons. August enjoyed that his days had a lot of variety and were each different.

The one thing you don't get with homeschooling is extracurricular activities. August was very interested in lacrosse and it happened that the school teams would let on homeschool students. August was added to the Davis Drive Middle School team, which was a bit awkward at first, but he soon got to know the other boys. As we had discussed with the previous psychiatrist, one of August's favorite things to do was to whack at things with sticks. From what I could tell, this was the main activity in lacrosse. He also had an insane stamina that would allow him to run forever without tiring and freakish hand/eye coordination. He was born for lacrosse. He took to it really quickly, having never played before. It was obvious that many of the boys had been playing for a while. What he lacked in knowledge of the game he definitely made up for in natural talent and sheer force of will. He wasn't happy that he didn't get to play the whole game because he doesn't get the concept of allowing everyone a chance to play. And he has enough stamina to play the whole game, which most kids wouldn't. I wasn't happy that some of those boys who were supposed to be middle schoolers looked old enough to have driven themselves there! The team did okay and August had a good time.

At the end of what would have been August's 7th grade year, I was required to get him tested to see how the schooling had gone. I found someone who conducted these tests and we got it done. After 1 ½ years of homeschooling he was behind, and he had already been behind when we started. It was hard to say if he was farther behind, just as behind, or if he'd caught up because we didn't know where he was before. But the result seemed to be that homeschooling wasn't a miracle pill for his education and it wasn't making a radical change in his behavior. We had a decision to make. Keep with the homeschooling and see if we could find a way to make it work better. Or put him back in school.

The decision was made to put him back into public school but have him repeat 7th grade. And we moved him from the magnet school he had been in to the base public school for our neighborhood. He hadn't been in the regular public school in our area for many years so we didn't think his being a year behind would be a problem. And we hoped that since he'd had 7th grade material while he'd been homeschooled that maybe it would be an easy year for him and it would go smoothly from both a learning and a behavioral standpoint.

Once again RAD was about to prove us so very wrong.

CHAPTER NINE

# Back in Public School

As we have done at the beginning of every school year, we started full of hope and optimism. A new school, new teachers, new administration. A chance to start fresh and, since we had decided to redo 7th grade, maybe with less pressure and anxiety. I had learned in the few short years with reactive attachment disorder that no matter how many setbacks we had, I had to keep hoping that our next attempt would be the right move. We would have found the right situation. But clearly, I still didn't understand completely how RAD works. Because he wasn't healing in any significant way. And the parts of his brain that were still broken weren't going to mend quickly if at all.

But what I did have now was more knowledge. Knowledge of how the school system works. Knowledge of August's rights and what I also was entitled to. And I was hopeful that armed with this increased knowledge, I could create an environment where August could be successful.

So, immediately, we set up both an IEP and a BIP. The IEP would allow for assistance with his educational needs so that we could keep him on task and hopefully get him interested if not excited about learning. The BIP was a behavioral intervention plan that would give him expectations but also outlets when his anxiety and frustrations got too overwhelming. I was most interested in this because I did have a concern that he might have some issues at going to a school where he was a grade behind his friends. His inflated ego I imagined would overcome that, and it proved to be right, but I wanted to anticipate everything.

Some things happen in your life that strengthen your resolve. They bring you closer to your family. You form a team to fight whatever life throws at you. You're a united front, and you approach each day as though nothing is impossible as long as you tackle it together.

But, sometimes, that doesn't work out so well. Sometimes, the struggles in your life break you and you can't find your way back to whatever felt like normal. You don't look broken and you don't act broken but you are. That's what happens when you're a parent of a child with reactive attachment disorder. A RAD parent has to grieve for the child that is fighting against loving them. They have to grieve for the potential you see in them that your child may not realize. And the heartbreak that comes with knowing the trauma your child endured in the past that has resulted in their tortured present.

These are the two paths of a family dealing with RAD. Unfortunately, ours went down the latter. After the stress of seven years of infertility, followed by two children in seven months then a cross-country move, my husband and I had been through a lot before August was even diagnosed. Before knowing exactly what we were dealing with, there had been more than a few rough patches as we discussed how to handle his behavioral issues.

After August's diagnosis, I became a warrior for him, getting him the treatment he needed, the education he was entitled to, and being his biggest fan. August's dad was a more traditional parent, which was fine, except we didn't have a traditional kid. The gap got wider and wider as August's issues got more and more intense. We retreated into our own corners, and I didn't know how to fix that. I was consumed with August and how to help him. I was also trying to make sure his brother didn't get lost in the chaos.

By Christmas, it was obvious that August's father and I weren't going to be able to mend our relationship. We made the decision to separate. We knew the boys had to be the first priority. We began mediation with lawyers and discussing how to make things as easy for the boys as possible. We decided to "nest" as a way to keep the boys in the house all the time. This meant that we got an apartment near the house and their father and I alternated living there and the house. The boys wouldn't have to shuffle between houses that way.

The time came to talk to the boys. We sat down all together in the family room and braced for crying and anger. We were both so scared of what the boys would say or do, particularly August, who already had issues of abandonment. We provided the news in the most comforting way possible, and August's response was, "I knew it. I was right! We get two rooms!" There may have been actual dancing. Needless to say, he wasn't pleased when we explained nesting and that, at least, in the beginning, he was only going to have the room he had now. But in the future, he would have two rooms, and that made him feel better. There was no emotion about the separation at all. I want to be clear that neither his father nor I blame August's RAD for the divorce.

By February, the separation had been worked out and we had managed to get into a routine that was working pretty well. I needed to think about getting a job, which I was working on, but things at school with August were continuing to decline. There were ongoing issues with his doing work and his attitude. His attitude at home wasn't any better. It didn't seem to have changed as a result of the separation. His relationship with the new therapist was fine, but there didn't seem to be any progress being made.

By May, it seemed like this year was shaping up to have been a disaster. He had failing grades and he didn't seem to care at all about it. And he was about to go out with a bang. August had brought a water bottle to school. But it didn't have water in it. No. It had vodka. He talked a couple of other boys into meeting him in the bathroom where of course they got caught. The school year had already gone so far downhill, I didn't think it could head any further into the ditch. Boy was I wrong.

Luckily, this time, there were no police involved. Again, he was able to catch a break. The county had a diversion program where, instead of an arrest, kids could spend a Saturday learning about the evils of alcohol and drugs. And that would take care of the issue.

Of course, with any of these consequences, it's a punishment for the parents as well. We also had to be present at the Saturday presentation. Maybe ten students and their grown-ups showed up that morning. All of the students looked like they'd rather be anywhere else. The parents all looked nervous. The facilitator went around and made every student tell the crowd exactly what they'd been busted for. That was fun. We then did some conversations, had some lectures, which I'm sure made no impact on the students. They talked about things like the damage to your brain from alcohol and drug use with fancy MRI pictures.

During a time when the parents were only meeting in the room the students were allowed to hang out outside, I found out recently in a conversation with August, that many of the kids smoked pot during this little break in their action. It was an effective use of our time.

After that, there was an in-school suspension with one teacher and one other student in one tiny room where he worked mostly on a computer. It might have been great if that could have been his way of doing school for the rest of middle school with fewer distractions. Then, the rest of the year was kind of a blur. Nothing much was accomplished due to no schoolwork and continued behavioral issues. And while I continued to make the efforts, it was clear that this year was achieving nothing. I don't know what the disconnect was for him. He was given so much support from teachers and administration, but he just didn't see how much we wanted him to be successful.

With less than adequate therapy and another failure in education, we were definitely at a crossroads in how to help August in a real, tangible way. And it seemed we were running out of options.

CHAPTER TEN

# Sending My Son Away

was at a loss. Where do I go from here? What is the magic pill that will heal my son? It was becoming more and more obvious that the solution—if there was one—didn't exist in our home, in a local school, or with a local therapist. I became a detective on the internet to learn about residential treatment centers for RAD. The thought scared me to death. Would he ever forgive me? Would I ever forgive myself? How would his brother handle it? Could we afford it if insurance wouldn't cover it? Could we afford not to? Nothing seemed certain except we were out of choices and needed a solution.

As I began to investigate, I got extremely frustrated. There were an amazing variety of residential treatment programs out there. Programs that are designed to scare a kid straight. Programs that focus on addiction treatment. Programs that don't focus on anything and will take on any psychiatric issue. I found nothing designed specifically for Reactive Attachment Disorder. Lots of programs existed in North Carolina but nothing that would help my son the way he needed help. There were no day treatment programs, nothing that our very good insurance could recommend. I looked for weeks. I found programs that included RAD on their list of disorders they would treat but I didn't want a place where he would also be with people dealing with addictions and bi-polar and schizophrenia, and eating disorders. I knew from looking for a therapist that the level of knowledge I was looking for wouldn't be at one of these places. The huge gap between unsuccessful weekly therapy appointments and nothing available for further treatment in the entire state I lived in, speaks volumes about the state of juvenile mental health in our nation.

Then I found it. It was like finding the pot of gold at the end of the rainbow. It was such an amazing feeling knowing that there was such a place. It was four states away in

Missouri and it was called Change Academy Lake of the Ozarks (CALO). Reading through the materials online it seemed too good to be true. It followed the methodology of Daniel Hughes. The doctor whose books I'd devoured whose treatment ideas made the most sense to me. The location enabled the residents to enjoy an amazing number of outdoor activities, which August would love, including boating, hiking, and camping. They used golden retrievers in their therapy and each resident got a dog that they trained and that stayed with them during their time there. They had an accredited school so August could keep up with his classes and hopefully catch up... What was I missing?

Oh yeah... the part where I'd have to send him away.

I talked about this with his father and with the therapist. We were all out of ideas of what to try next. It did seem counterintuitive to send away a child who had abandonment issues. But there was family therapy built into the treatment plan and we were encouraged to come visit as often as possible. Still, without being completely sure this was the right decision, August's father and I flew to Missouri to see what CALO was all about.

It's almost a two-hour drive from the airport to the facility. I found out later that it used to be a "fat farm" for wives of Hallmark executives back in the day. That made me giggle. What a different purpose now! It's tucked away among very expensive resort homes of the wealthy who I imagine may not even know what goes one there. It's not a gated or locked down place, something that will come into play later in our story. There's a small sign that leads you down an unassuming gravel road to a locked door of a building that could be a church camp or boy scout camp. When we went in, we were given some generic materials about the place, how the treatment is laid out, bios of the executive staff, their philosophy, etc. We met with several of the staff who oversaw various parts of operations: education, therapy, counselors.

Then we got ready to go on a tour. Right as we went into the main room, which was used as a social room, a number of counselors were having to restrain a boy who was obviously having problems. The boy was face down on the floor and there was a counselor on top of him holding him still and others holding his arms. Now, he was a big guy, twice the size of my little August. I almost turned around right there. I know that these kids can have those kinds of rages; I've dealt with them myself. But it's different when you think about someone else putting their hands on your son.

Off the social room, after the dust settled, we got to see the bedrooms. Each room had two beds with drawers underneath. The boys can have their own bedding. They also have room for crates for their dogs when they get them and a closet each and a shared bathroom. The bathroom has a door but there's no door to the room. There are two floors of rooms. There's a classroom with computers; all learning is done online, and they can move at their own pace. It's an accredited program, so they can transfer everything they do to whatever school they go to when they leave. There's art therapy with a full-time art therapist. There are sensory rooms with several different options. In the middle of the social area in what used to be a therapy pool is a rock wall. There are couches spread out around the room with TVs that show movies. There are girls on the other side of the building and they are always kept separated. There's a nice cafeteria. The counselors have offices of their own on the second floor. And the lake is a short walk away.

After the tour we sat down with the director and learned

about the treatment program. Everything made sense to me. Following the treatment protocols of Daniel Hughes, which I understood from reading; it made sense in this environment. My head made sense of everything I was hearing. The price tag was steep; $10,500 a month. We were told that insurance might cover 4-6 months; that was the average of what they have seen. After that we could appeal and maybe get another month or two. So maybe we'd get six months with him there. And they couldn't say of course what effect that would have. Would that be enough?

But there was my heart. I'm considering sending my son away. Is it because I think I'm doing what's best for him? Or am I just fed up? Am I just wanting CALO to be better than it really is? How do I reconcile my head and my heart and make a decision that is going to change our lives so drastically? And will he ever forgive me?

We made the decision to move forward. It seemed like the right thing to do. We had no more options in our area. We didn't see a next step in North Carolina. So now it came down to when and how to tell August. None of that was going to be easy. On any of us.

I honestly don't remember telling August about his going to CALO. I can only hope that it means that it went smoothly and there was no crying or screaming or rages. We made the decision to have him start in September when he'd normally be starting school. We began the process of figuring out what he'd need. We let him be involved in as many of the decisions as we could.

We also worked with the insurance company on getting approval for his placement. Because of course insurance companies don't want to pay a dollar more than they have to, CALO had to call and get approval EVERY WEEK for August to stay. More on that later.

At last, the day came to go. The combination of feelings I had can't even be explained. I kept telling myself it was the right thing to do, alternating with it being a great new adventure for August along with our family needing the break (I hated that one). In the end, I kept the hope that we were making the right decision. I don't know if I were reassuring myself or trying to convince myself...

We arrived in Lake of the Ozarks Missouri the night before we were to drop August off. We found a resort hotel that would become our base of operations every time we came to town in the future. We acted as if some life-changing event wasn't happening the next morning. The elephant in the room couldn't have been larger.

The next morning, we drove over to CALO with August and all his possessions. My nerves were on fire. I didn't know how he would react. I didn't know how I would react. I knew I needed to keep my brave face on for him, but I wasn't sure I had it in me. We were met by the department heads, who were very gracious. They took August's suitcase to put in storage and remove the few things that he's allowed to have, which isn't much. Mostly the clothing and shoes are stored for when he's allowed off campus.

August went off on a tour while we finished some paperwork and then we met up with him. We found his room and helped him make his bed. We found the dogs and walked down to the lake. We then went and talked to the school teacher. August, not surprisingly went off and found the video games. I sat with him for a while and tried to get him to talk about what he saw and what he thought of the place. He didn't say much. I tried to get him to talk to me about how he was feeling about staying there. Again, not much. I told him we were getting ready to leave and that I would miss him horribly, but we would talk on the phone and Skype. I asked him how he felt about that. His reply burns in my heart all these years later, "If you're not taking me with you, then just go."

I cried all the way home.

## CHAPTER ELEVEN

# *August is Gone*

got back home to find my water heater had exploded and all the carpet in my condo had to be replaced. It also meant black mold had gotten into the wall behind my bathroom cabinet and that wall which is shared with the boys' bedroom had to be torn out and repaired along with the cabinet. The expense was enormous, but it was secondary to how it piled on to the already overwhelming feeling of my life falling down around me.

We weren't allowed to talk to August for the first couple of weeks he was there so he could get adjusted to his new environment and routines. It felt like forever before we could see him. This happened in the first Google Hangout call we had with him and his therapist. The goal of these calls was family therapy; August could begin the process of recognizing his past trauma, and we could begin to learn the words and tools to help him deal with those feelings in a more positive way.

The technology wasn't like it is today. There weren't ten ways to do a video call. Our best choice was a Google Hangout which required a perfectly sunny day and the most robust internet connection we could muster. We tried initially with August's dad and I in our respective locations but it became clear after the first couple of times that it worked better if we limited the number of locations we were trying to connect. So, he would come to my office and we would have the calls together.

The first therapist August had wasn't the best match. He tried much too hard to be August's friend. He didn't confront August's beliefs as much as I would have liked. And while he offered up some of the issues that we needed to deal with, he didn't follow through on digging deeper in the discussions. The therapy ended up being more of a video visit.

I went out to see August for Thanksgiving. It was surreal to see him in that space. He'd made some friends after a couple of months and was settled in. He was loving having the therapy dogs around. He didn't like school or therapy, but he did like watching TV. Not much of a change from home. We were able to eat Thanksgiving dinner together on campus. I wasn't able to take him off campus at that point.

At Christmas, we all met in Lake of the Ozarks and had a weird and wonderful family Christmas. We were able to take August off campus. Unfortunately, he couldn't have much there, so we couldn't give him presents of any sort. But the time together was worth the trip.

Around this time, we also got our first insurance denial. We'd had a few conversations with the insurance folks prior to this but this was their first big "NO." The insurance processing required that it be filed weekly, so every week we had to hold our breath and see if it got approved. We'd gotten through four months, which was what CALO told us to expect, and, sure enough, right at that point, they said no. The appeal process generally involved the therapist getting on the phone with a doctor from the insurance company and explaining the treatment he's been receiving and why it needed to continue. I didn't think that was enough. I insisted we be in on the phone call. And just like before, I wrote another letter detailing August's entire history in order to make perfectly clear why CALO was where he needed to be and why staying there was necessary.

The day came for the phone call. August's dad and I, the therapist and the insurance doctor all got on the phone. The doctor asked a couple questions about August's treatment which the therapist answered. Once again, my letter, outlining everything we'd tried for treating August and everything he'd been through was the thing that clinched it. The insurance rep said based on that write up he understood that August's treatment had been exhausted locally and that CALO was the right place for him and granted the appeal. The administration at CALO said we were so rare in getting continuing coverage.

Things got even more interesting in January. I had an extended business trip traveling to several of my company's locations doing interviews for new staff. I landed in Boston late, with the plan to get to a hotel, pick up termination documents and terminate an employee in the morning, then hold interviews for that position and fly back home after almost three weeks on the road. Upon touching down and turning on my phone, it blew up with messages.

August had run away. In January. In the hills of Missouri. While CALO isn't a gated facility one of the things they do to deter things like running is that no one gets shoes. They get socks and shower shoes-like sandals. And no one has jackets. Everyone gets at most a t-shirt and sweatshirt. So, in the dead of winter at night, my son is outside in a sweatshirt and shower shoes.

After all these years, just writing that previous paragraph still makes my heart hurt and makes my anxiety level rise. I was on the back of a plane full of people in Boston, Massachusetts. My distressed, psychologically fragile child was out in the freezing winter weather, 1,500 miles away. I have never felt more helpless in my entire life. Just to add insult to injury when I finally got off the plane and got to baggage claim my suitcase was missing.

Luckily, I was traveling with a co-worker who got me out of the airport and to the hotel. I have no memory of that block of time. I might have been making phone calls to CALO, to

August's dad. Not really sure. I know once I got to the hotel, I called my sister. I asked her to put out a prayer request. I called the airlines to see what the earliest flight to St. Louis was. I don't know if I called my dad. I can't remember what time it was. I knew I should probably try to sleep if I was going to need to go to St. Louis in a few hours but that seemed unlikely.

When you have these hours alone during a crisis with your child somewhere and you don't know what the outcome is going to be...I can't describe what goes on in your mind. It's like what people say when you have a near-death experience and your life flashes in front of your eyes. But this time it's not your life. It's your child's. August's life came to me in waves. All the good and all the bad. Ten years of loving this child and being his cheerleader and working so hard to help him heal and grow. And in this moment trying my hardest not to let myself think that today is the day that all those memories stop.

Somewhere in the couple of hours that went by, I dozed off. And then I got the call that he'd been found. August and the boys he'd left with had finally gotten too cold and decided they'd had enough. In the relatively few hours they'd been gone, they had managed to break into a car and find a gun. They'd hooked up with some girls and went to their apartment and smoked some pot. They'd broken into a warehouse, pulled out some insulation and lit it on fire to get warm and August had gone to the bathroom in the company's front yard. All the trespassing on the company property was caught on video tape. They were extremely active in the hours they were gone.

Figuring out what happened and why would be a process. There was law enforcement involvement because they broke into the car and the warehouse and did damage to the warehouse. There were conversations with the therapists individually before I could talk to him. When I did get to hear his voice, all I wanted to know was that he was safe. I couldn't level any consequences. Asking him what he had been thinking wouldn't accomplish anything.

But I couldn't do the thing I needed to do. When your son is hurting so much that he does something like run away, you're so scared you just want them back. When he's found, yes, you want to shake him till his teeth rattle because you were so mad that he scared you. But mostly, you just want to hug him till he gasps for breath. That's what I couldn't do. I couldn't hug him, stroke his hair, kiss his cheeks, or scratch his back. I couldn't make sure he knew that whatever he did, even something as bonehead stupid as what he'd just done, that the hugs, hair stroking, kisses, and back scratching would still happen no matter what.

As would prove the case through his life later on, August got away with it. No charges were filed, and he was put on essentially probation for 12 months. He was on restrictions at CALO for a while. If he felt any remorse for what he'd put his father, me, and the staff through, he hid it well. Soon after that, we got a new therapist.

The new therapist proved to be a game-changer. She wouldn't let August cruise through therapy sessions. She called him on all the crap he tried to pull. She forced him to answer questions rather than dodge the hard stuff. She got in his face. And she worked with his school teacher and the other staff to make sure he wasn't getting away with anything.

That would have been enough for your average RAD kid. But time had already proven that August wasn't the average

RAD kid. So, in turn, over the next couple months, he stepped up his game. He and his friends learned how to set off the smoke alarms even when they had no access to open flames. He swallowed magnets in the Spring, which sent him to the hospital for an x-ray to make sure they would pass and not connect in his intestines requiring surgery. He found a way around CALO's firewall which allowed him to play internet games and search for inappropriate sites during school. And he engaged in some sort of still unknown sexual interaction with another male student which he says was unwanted and required a report and investigation by Missouri Child Services. And let's not forget that, at this point, he's only been there about six months.

We had to have a serious discussion with the therapist because they were very close to kicking him out. What runs through a mother's mind when the place of last resort tells you they don't think they can help your child? Complete and total panic. As much fear as I had already lived through, it was nothing compared to what began to build in my heart and head in the month as we discussed with August and the therapist what needed to be done in order for him to stay. We explained to him the situation. We tried to get him to believe in the benefits of being there. We tried to implore with him to want to help himself. Then we waited to see what would happen next.

August had a therapy dog named Destiny. Destiny was very high-strung and hard to handle. It had been frustrating for August training her because of that. August made the decision that he needed to separate from Destiny and be matched with a new dog. He picked Mia. Mia couldn't be more laid back if she were on medication. She was calm and attentive and smart and so easy to train. August was able to work with her and, in no time, he and Mia had gotten their

AKC certification and Mia was a full-fledged therapy dog. Mia went with us everywhere to the movies, shopping, to restaurants, you name it. And August was so proud of how Mia behaved. Were it not for Mia's extreme car sickness this would have been perfect.

Around Independence Day, August's brother and I went on vacation and we went out to visit August. Things had gotten progressively better. We took him off campus for a few days and had a good time over the holiday weekend. He'd gotten the message about needing to "get with the program," and he was starting to put in the work. Unfortunately, I would be back by myself the next weekend to pick him up and take him with me to Indiana for the funeral of my grandmother, his great-grandmother, whom, as much as it was possible for August, he dearly loved. When we brought August home and he learned English, he decided for himself that he wanted to be called August and not "Goose" or "Goosya," which was his Russian nickname. His great-grandmother was the only one he wouldn't correct when she continued to use those names. He loved going to visit her and spending time talking with her. He never objected when she asked him to help her, and I truly treasured that bond, tenuous though it was, that they had built. When I showed up just a week after having been there, August knew exactly what had happened before I said a word. Without the actual coping skills and true ability to feel the feelings, he didn't exhibit the sadness I'm sure was there. It made the time for me even sadder watching him.

As summer crept into Fall August continued to progress and looked like he was going to actually get through the CALO program. It appeared like he would be graduating by Christmas. He was doing well in school, his behavior had leveled off, he was handling Mia well, and our therapy sessions, while not creating major breakthroughs, were at least productive and valuable.

We moved closer to Christmas and to August graduating from CALO and coming home. CALO did a great thing in doing an actual "graduation" of sorts for him by having all the boys come to an event. August and his therapist and his father and I spoke about his time there and how proud we were of all he'd accomplished. They even let him link in by computer a friend who'd already gone home. Afterward, we packed up all his things, including Mia. We dropped Dad at the airport and went to spend Christmas at my grandmother's house in Indiana where my aunt was still living and the tradition of gathering there was hard to break. August's father's father had gone into the hospital shortly before our trip to CALO and while we were at grandma's, I got the call that he had passed away. I wasn't at all happy to have to be the one to relay the news again about the passing of a relative to August and his brother. We finished our visit and set off for North Carolina. August's first experience back in the world would be his grandfather's funeral. Not a great reentry. It would be strange having August back home after 16 months away. It was like adopting him all over again.

## CHAPTER TWELVE

# Back Home Again

We settled back into our every other week rotation. The boys spent one week with their dad and one week with me. Mia also traveled back and forth, which made for more interesting weekly hand offs. We had made some inquiries into schools for August and were pretty sure we had found a good match, but, of course, we wanted August to visit before we made a final decision. We weren't pushing to get him enrolled right after the holidays. We had toured a couple of places before August got home and knew things that would be deal breakers for him: uniforms, religious schools, no sports. We took August to a school we thought would meet our needs and his as well. The Fletcher Academy was designed for students who, from mostly a behavioral standpoint, just didn't thrive in a mainstream school environment. The class sizes were small, he could advance somewhat as he was able, and they had sports teams. He seemed agreeable to the place and plans were made to get him enrolled.

This first included a "shadow day" which he spent following a student of his own grade to see what it was like. He made friends almost immediately. August's charm continued to amaze me. To this day, wishing he put that charisma to good use has always been my dream because there's no telling what he could do!

He started school, and, since it was January, it was basketball season. One of the first days, we stayed after to watch a game. He begged me to help him get on the team (in a school this small, anyone who wants to can play). He needed an athletic physical which we managed to get a couple days later. By Friday of his first week of school, August was on the Fletcher Academy basketball team and one of their better players.

August seemed to settle into school well. The first year, he did well in his classes. We weren't having a lot of big blow ups at home. He'd even met a girl whom he liked. We had a honeymoon period that made us think just maybe Fletcher would be the academic answer we'd been searching for. Just maybe it was the breakthrough that was going to bring back the sweet boy we'd brought home from Russia.

The Fall of the next year coincided with the hiring of a new principal. The previous principal had a good rapport with August and could get him back on track when he started to misbehave without making him angry. The new one didn't get August and immediately labeled him a bad guy (see teacher match!)

August continued his streak of being able to find the kid in any school who is the worst possible influence. This was a boy from Germany whose name I've blocked out. But the two of them together got into more trouble in a shorter amount of time than I thought possible. We found videos of them smoking (just cigarettes at this point thankfully) on his phone. They both signed up to play soccer and then both got kicked off the soccer team. School started to become more of a battle.

And things were about to get more complicated.

My world got severely rocked. I got laid off from my job of four years. I feverishly looked for another position in Raleigh but that wasn't resulting in much success. Simultaneously, my aunt who had been living with my grandmother in Indiana was in the process of putting the farm my grandparents had lived in since I was four on the market. She wanted to move to Cincinnati to be closer to her kids and grandkids. On a whim, I looked for jobs there, in Terre Haute, Indiana. I found one working with the American Cancer Society, applied, and was hired. It would enable me to buy my grandparent's house and keep that small farm, which had been my family's "happy place" for over 40 years, in the family and be a new beginning for me. But now what to do about the boys?

I first talked to the boys' father. He made it quite clear that he would fight me for custody if I tried to take them to Indiana. I didn't expect anything different. And I don't know if I could have won because I was unemployed and broke and living in a two-bedroom condo and he had a six-figure income and was living in a four-bedroom house. I couldn't afford the fight he could. Then I talked to August's brother. He was excited about my living on the farm and us keeping it. He also really liked his school in North Carolina. And quite frankly the schools in Terre Haute couldn't hold a candle to the education he was getting and would continue to get in Raleigh. My heart was breaking at the thought of not seeing them every day, but it was the right decision, and I really had no choice. I was going to move to Indiana and the boys were going to stay in North Carolina.

The boys love the farm. I thought of course they would love the idea of my keeping it in the family. And I wasn't even sure they would get what my being so far away would mean. August was in a good place at the moment and Spencer was happy in his school. It seemed like the best possible time to do something for me. After 10 years of having been a stay-at-home mom, I was going to have a job I was truly passionate about and live in a home that I loved. And I'd still be a mother to my children, knowing they were being cared for by their father, who was an excellent parent. We had a couple months to figure out how this was all going to work out, so we talked more and made plans.

The boys would come up at Christmas and Spring Break and

for the Summer. I got them both Kindles for Christmas so we could Skype (this was before the invention of the phone with FaceTime) whenever we wanted to. I did everything to make sure the connections between us remained. Then, in January, I moved 600 miles away from my boys.

For a while, things seemed to go just fine. Skype, phone calls, texting kept us in touch. The boys came to visit for Spring break. They even helped me with my first Relay for Life event! August continued to do okay at Fletcher and added Frisbee football to his list of sports. Spencer was loving middle school. When school was out for the summer, they came to the farm, and we had a great time. They each took a room which they started to make their own. I had my first Independence Day family reunion, continuing a tradition that my grandparents had started when they first moved to the farm 40 years earlier. But now it was my turn as hostess, and it felt good to put my stamp on it with the boys' help.

At the end of the summer, the boys went back to North Carolina and school started. August started playing soccer at school again. And then once again, things started going off the rails. He was having discipline problems at school. He and his father were butting heads regularly. The school situation with August finally came to a head and he was expelled from Fletcher in November. There was a rumor that he had snuck off with his new girlfriend on school property and had sex. This was something he supposedly bragged about to other kids at school along with detailed descriptions of sex acts. There was also a rumor that he had gotten his new girlfriend pregnant. The new headmaster had a zero tolerance for any sexual misconduct, which he felt he was obligated to, given that some of the kids at the school had sexual trauma in their backgrounds. So, he was out. Let's ponder this...the school that's designed to work with students with behavioral issues kicked out my son for his behavioral issues. Yep. Couple that with the ever-declining relationship with his father and it became clear that August wasn't going to be able to stay in North Carolina. We discussed it and I agreed he needed to come live with me. There were a couple of alternative high schools in Terre Haute which might be good choices. Plus, I had always been able to stay calmer where August's behavior was concerned.

Plans were made and August moved up to Terre Haute with me. August and I were now faced with how we were going to navigate this new version of our relationship.

## CHAPTER THIRTEEN

# The Move to Terre Haute

He'd made it at the school designed for kids like him about six school months altogether. We made plans to get him up to me and I started the conversation with the Vigo County School Corporation on getting him enrolled in school. I tried to impress upon them that he needed to go straight to the alternative school environment that they offered. It was much like Fletcher but not private, part of the public school system. I gave them the whole story. I told them all the gory details. I held back nothing. I had all his records. I told them about the residential treatment. But they felt like they wanted to take a shot at working with him and create an environment that hopefully he could be successful in. I should have fought more. When you have a child with RAD, by the time they are a teenager you know what will work. You've seen it all. You can predict the outcomes. Because the education system, no matter what the school district, isn't prepared to handle a RAD kiddo if you have to explain what RAD is. But I gave in and agreed, and we decided that we would start him in 10th grade in Terre Haute North High School.

August moved up to Terre Haute and he started school. He had turned 16 the previous March but hadn't yet gotten his driver's license so he was stuck taking the bus. I agreed to pick him up in the afternoon when I could. School wasn't terribly far away. He had an IEP which would allow for some additional time taking tests. He had the ability to take a "time out" if he felt emotionally overwhelmed and needed to take a break. But I was working a job where I had to travel a lot, have afternoon and evening meetings and meetings out of Terre Haute which left him home alone. It became evident very quickly that August was going to test his freedoms. The questions were how often and how far he was willing to go.

The answers to those questions came pretty fast. His streak

continued for finding the kids in any crowd who could get him in the most trouble. Terre Haute proved no different. The first boy he met seemed like a nice kid. He had manners and was well-behaved when I let him spend the night. But one afternoon they were in August's room, and I smelled pot through the vents wafting into my room. Now, I've never done drugs, but I went to college and know the smell. I went flying downstairs and into his room and there they were. Smoking and sitting by the open window. The kid actually told me August said I was cool with it. August looked at me like he wanted me to back him up to save face with his friend. What planet is this child on? We immediately went to the car, and I took the boy home. I didn't tell his parents, but I told him that he had to because he wasn't coming to our house anymore and he had to tell his parents why. And if they called me, I was going to tell the truth.

August was furious with me. This is one part of RAD I'll never understand. I do the proper parenting thing, and he gets mad at me. I had already confiscated the weed which was now hidden up in my room. August made a big deal about threatening to call the cops on me because if they found the pot in my room, I would be arrested. He thought that was the way to get back at me. I told him I was pretty sure they would know the situation once I explained it. But I was quick to dump it later that evening! I didn't trust him a bit.

We weren't done with the little things yet. He got nailed for smoking during welding class, which is, in fact, a misdemeanor and a fine of over $100, which I had to go to the courthouse and pay. The detentions piled up like Fall leaves for missed work and attitude and going in the girls' bathroom and a host of other infractions.

Then we had our first (but far from last) experience with the

Juvenile Justice system. It was customary for me to rent cars when I traveled for work because the cost was cheaper than paying mileage on my car. I had gone to an event in another county and gotten home late one evening to find my car and August gone. Remember, August didn't have a driver's license yet. It was a complicated process to convince the Indiana BMV that my son with the Russian birth certificate was a U.S. citizen, and we hadn't yet been successful. But he had still taken my car and hadn't yet come home. I did what I absolutely didn't want to do. I called the police. A sheriff came out (I live in the county not the city limits) and got all the information. I waited up as long as I could and when I couldn't stay awake, I did the next thing I never thought I'd do. I locked the door.

When August came home in the morning and knocked on the door, I looked at him and told him I wasn't letting him in. I called the sheriff's office and told them he was back. My neighbor had seen him trying to get in through the window and called me to let me know he'd thrown something in the bushes. When the sheriff arrived, they had the dogs search the bushes but just found his T-shirt. August was in the garage keeping warm in a sleeping bag. They cuffed him and took him away. I went inside and sobbed.

A couple hours later, he called. We talked about what had happened. He was a strange combination of remorseful and pissed. I was allowed to go down later and see him. There was a woman who talked with us about what had happened and what I wanted to do. Running away is a crime here. She really wanted me to also charge him with stealing my car. I couldn't bring myself to go there. If I only knew what lay ahead. Maybe if I had been more harsh then...

August stayed at the Juvenile detention center. I was allowed to visit him on weekends. This was the beginning of learning how having a child caught up in the criminal justice system consumes your life physically, mentally, emotionally. I had to learn how the system works. I had to plan my schedule (which luckily was flexible) around court dates, visitations with August, and meetings with his probation officer. I had to not let my "mama bear" emotions get in the way of figuring out if what might happen in the criminal justice system might be a good learning experience for him. All of this was swirling at the same time.

He was ultimately placed on probation, which, in August's ears, was like nothing had happened. Within months, he had been arrested for marijuana possession just over the border in Marshall, Illinois. By October he had committed so many probation violations that his probation officer tried to get the message through by putting him in juvenile detention for 30 days.

That had quite the impact (all sarcasm intended) because, by November, he was arrested for sexual assault of a minor. Now I need to take a pause here because that sounds a lot more horrible than it was. He had consensual sex with a girl who was legally underage. Her mom found out and decided to press charges. We had used a public defender prior to this, but now, it was time to get serious, so we hired a lawyer. And I learned a little more about the criminal justice system. And a lot more about people.

One thing I learned is that some people will never try to understand a situation no matter how many times you explain it to them. That's not an excuse for anything; it's just reality. In this case, it came in the form of the girl's mom, the mom's son, and the girl showing up one night in our driveway. I wasn't sure what was going on until I heard the dog bark and went outside to see August yelling, the mom yelling, and the two boys getting closer and closer. I thought I was in some made-for-TV movie. I quickly made August go inside. I didn't know this family. They didn't know me. They didn't know August for that matter. And whatever had gone wrong between her daughter and my son at this moment they were trespassing on my property and threatening my son. I made those points repeatedly. I won't ever make excuses for the behaviors of my child. But you can be damned sure I'll defend him with my life. I mean really...

This became the first time I ever introduced August's RAD into a conversation with anyone connected to the criminal justice system (teen court not truly being the justice system). I mentioned it to his lawyer, and he asked me to write him an explanation. I hadn't even talked about it with his probation officer who I'd now had an almost year-long relationship with. I'm not entirely sure why, except that it didn't seem like it would matter or change what was happening or needed to happen. Similar to filing for the insurance appeal, I wrote the three-page summary of his adoption history, diagnosis, what reactive attachment disorder is, how it manifests, and how it might affect him in the situations he's been in. Again, the lawyer said it was the most comprehensive write-up he'd ever gotten. I reminded him it wasn't my first rodeo. When you live with RAD, you spend a lot of time explaining it.

This would be the first Christmas August would spend behind bars. He was 17 and it was 2015. No Christmas presents. No waking up at home on Christmas morning. After opening presents with Spencer, I got dressed and went down to juvenile detention and spent two hours at a round table with my son with a guard in the room. Talking about everything and nothing. It wasn't the last. He would be behind bars for Christmas every year after.

## CHAPTER FOURTEEN

# August Turns 18

August got out in time for his 18th birthday. We had a plan to get together and have dinner and I was going to take him clothes shopping. After he got out of juvenile detention, he didn't have many clothes that fit. He'd gotten arrested right after he got out in January for illegal possession of alcohol, and I'd had to pick him up at 3 am. Things between us hadn't been going well. He wasn't staying at home much. He didn't like my rules.

I was trying to keep him in school but that was a race against time because as soon as he turned 18, I didn't have a say anymore. We were looking at moving him to an alternative school with smaller classes which might be a better fit (the place I wanted him to go all along) but I couldn't get him to come with me to visit and do the enrollment. I was slowly turning my attention to pursuing a GED route. I knew he could probably pass the test with very little studying and coursework. Maybe I could make that tradeoff if I told him there was going to be no more high school...

His birthday turned out to be a disaster. I'm not sure what had him so on edge, but he was so angry and argumentative. He wanted to go to a store that was closing in 10 minutes. I told him that wasn't fair to the people who worked there, and we could go back another day. But he insisted we go that day. He didn't want to go someplace for dinner. He just wanted to hit a drive-thru. We went to Wal-Mart to get him a few things. Then I dropped him off. It was awful. I had wanted a nice evening out with my son and instead I got this angry, mean short drive-by with someone I hardly recognized.

Turning 18 also meant I had no control over whether he went to school or not. I made another ultimatum that changed our relationship greatly. I told him that if he wasn't going to school full-time or getting a job, he wasn't staying at my house. He chose to leave.

His birthday is in March and the days that followed didn't get much better. He moved from place to place, getting in touch whenever he needed something: money, laundry, food. Mostly money. He was couch surfing and, occasionally, completely homeless. He'd call me or his dad with the most amazing story about how he was going to be killed, robbed, or frozen to death. His powers of manipulation were really honed during this time. At one point, his father got him a hotel room for a week with the condition that he use the time to find himself a more permanent solution. He told his dad he had a referral on a job. He didn't show up for the job and eventually got kicked out of the hotel for having wild parties.

Then things changed between us in April. I got a call from him in jail. He'd been arrested.

Breaking and entering is the charge. Apparently, he and some friends broke into an abandoned house to stay warm or something. Since he was 18 now, we were no longer dealing with juvenile court. We were in adult court. This was as serious as it gets. He got a public defender. I went to court to see what happened. He came in with an orange jumpsuit shackled to other inmates. Because of his youth and it being a first offense and some other miracles only August seems to find, he got probation.

He came home and things weren't any better. There was no option to get him to a doctor or a therapist, so there was no medication. He was angry all the time. When he didn't get what he wanted, the rages were intense and there was no more, "hold him till he likes it." He was never dangerously physical with me, but grabbing my arm or throwing his phone in my direction was enough to make me afraid.

Of course, just getting probation didn't do much to get him scared straight because a month later he was arrested for "conversion," which was selling stolen goods. He wasn't out again this time as quickly.

When he did get out, we communicated very little. Again, if he wanted money or food, he got in touch. He always made it seem like he was about to die. He owed somebody money and they were going to kill him if he didn't get money. He left me handwritten notes on the back porch because I had the locks changed to keep him from coming in and stealing from me. I wrote him notes back.

But my life was falling apart. I couldn't do my job. I couldn't get out of bed many days. I was terrified of his showing up at the house. I was terrified of his friends. I was terrified every time I knew he'd been to the house when I wasn't there.

In September, two things happened. He stole my car again, and I finally did what I should have done the first time. I had him arrested for stealing my car. And I took out an order of protection and eviction against my own son.

He texted me, begging and pleading with me not to have him charged for the car. I still have screen shots of the conversation. He said they just drove it back behind my property. So technically, it wasn't stolen if it was still on my land. I didn't even know he had a key. He knew this was going to be a big deal. But I had to go through with it. I couldn't let him get away with treating me like he had been. The manipulation and the lack of respect and the flat-out fear of what might happen next had to stop. The fear that what physical confrontations we had had might escalate couldn't be ignored. I had to take care of me. Even if it meant doing harm to what was left of my relationship with August.

After the arrest, I went to visit the people at CODA...the Council on Domestic Abuse. I'd never even considered what I'd been experiencing as abuse, but I knew I needed something to change, and I wanted to talk to someone. They were the only people I could think of. There, I learned about taking out an order of protection. The very helpful and kind woman walked me through what was involved, asked me some questions about my situation, and I learned that, indeed, I was in an abusive situation with August. I told the stories and said the words out loud. All the help I'd tried to give him had landed me here. On the receiving end of trying to get help for myself to protect me from him.

The paperwork was filed and on September 15th with August also there in court, I again told the stories and said the words out loud. And I was granted an order of protection and eviction against my own son. Then I went home and cried harder than I thought was possible.

Somehow, August was back out on the street soon after all this, in time to get another possession of marijuana and conversion charge in October. I wasn't part of this one, so I don't know what happened other than he spent another Christmas in jail.

He got out in early 2017 in time to catch another conversion charge in March and a receiving stolen auto parts charge in April. With some amount of dumb luck, he was able to get sentenced to work release. His father and I spent about $250 to get him the required items that he had to have to live in the work release facility. He moved there in June. His first time going out was June 16th. And if all of what you've read so far has you hanging your mouth open, just you wait.

## CHAPTER FIFTEEN

# *Another Run Away*

August never returned from work release. Even writing that sentence now it surprises me that it surprised me. He was given such a gift with that opportunity but like all second, third, fourth, tenth chances, he wasn't going to take the road to redemption. He was going to try and take what he thought would be the easy way out. So now my son was a fugitive. Now there was no active man hunt. But they were looking for him.

Because he'd essentially escaped from jail. Even though they'd let him out, he was supposed to return and he didn't. I never saw him the entire time he was gone. I never saw him until he got caught again.

That happened two weeks later on June 30th, right before all my family was due to come to my house for Independence Day weekend. I checked Facebook and found sympathy messages from a couple of friends because August's mugshot was in the local paper as one of the people arrested in connection with a local armed robbery of a convenience store the night before. Well, I know where he is now.

I let his dad know what had happened. And I waited for the phone call.

## CHAPTER SIXTEEN

# My Son Goes to Prison

This isn't going to be one that the public defender can handle. So once again we shell out the big bucks for the power lawyer to the tune of $25,000. This is reactive attachment disorder. After everything the child has done to you, all the heartbreak and physical and emotional hurt, there's no bottom. August is our child, and we'll do anything for him.

I sit down with the lawyer and get the full story. August and a few other people were present at an armed robbery. The store clerk was shot, but August didn't do it. The store clerk lived. They all ran, and, in the course of trying to get away somewhere, they apparently tried to steal a car when August pointed a gun at the car owner. They were eventually caught. August was looking at multiple felonies and misdemeanors, and, if the DA was feeling cranky, possibly attempted murder.

I consider myself a relatively intelligent person but the words he was speaking sounded like a foreign language to me or like he was talking about someone else. Of course, this escalation was inevitable. Wasn't it? Should I have seen this coming? Am I somehow to blame? When could I have done something to keep this from happening? So many thoughts swirling in my head that I thought my brain would just explode.

But mostly what I thought was this: *What had happened to my sweet, beautiful bright-eyed boy? Where had his miswired brain led him that I couldn't correct that path?* Obviously, not every child with RAD ends up like August, but the lack of trust that RAD eats away in these children means they can go in so many different directions. And it left August so hard and unfeeling that he saw this as a better choice.

The lawyer was able to negotiate a reduced sentence if August were willing to do some work as well. A twelve-year sentence could be reduced to eight years and then reduced even more if he were willing to show some behavioral work, things like taking a course and trying to finish his GED. He reluctantly agreed. But I could tell the wheels were already spinning on how to manipulate that system.

He stayed at the local jail for a while because space was unavailable in the place where they go next before being assigned to their permanent location. I was able to visit through video calls. Very impersonal set up in a row of machines with others doing the same thing. There were no in-person visits at all.

Then, one day, he was gone with no notice. The clearing facility, which was about an hour away, didn't allow visits or calls, so, for a month, there was no contact. Then I found out he'd been placed at the Putnamville Correctional Facility, just a 35-minute drive from me. Now it was time to learn how to be a mom with a kid in prison.

First, you have to learn how to communicate. There's a third-party system that allows you to add your phone number and put money on so that your person can call your number only. That way, August couldn't use those funds to call just anyone; he could only call me. I liked that a lot. His dad had to do the same thing with his phone number.

Second, there was a commissary account into which you could deposit money so he could get extra food, snacks, and stuff. It wasn't necessary but, over time, August was insistent he'd starve to death without extra food. His dad and I agreed to alternate $20 a week on that.

Lastly, there was an account we could fund that would give him money to order music and movies onto the tablet each person was issued. This tablet was also how he could email me and make phone calls. There would be more drama surrounding this tablet down the road.

All this I figured out fairly easily. Then I had to navigate the wild world of getting to visit him. This was much less straightforward. There was an online form to fill out. It wasn't terribly complicated for me, but more involved for his dad, brother, and my sister because if you're from out of state, you have to supply actual copies of your driver's licenses. Being in-state, I could get away with just putting in the number. But the form was fairly intense and asked a lot of questions.

Then it came back that I was denied because of the order of protection. We weren't allowed to be in the same place. Rats. I had to get that lifted. So, I had to figure out how to do that. Turned out it wasn't terrible, just filing a piece of paper; didn't even have to go to court myself. Whew! The facility got notified that the order had been lifted. Then I had to reapply; well, that bites. Couldn't they just use my initial application, knowing the situation had changed? Of course not.

New application entered. More waiting. Finally, about three weeks later, it was approved, and I could visit. So began one of the most entertaining and terrifying adventures I've ever been on.

The list of do's and don'ts to visit an inmate is pretty lengthy, even more so for women. And on my first visit, I missed a lot of them. I knew I couldn't bring my cell phone. I knew I couldn't have any jewelry. But I missed the part about no sleeveless shirts. After walking all the way from the distant parking lot, I was turned around and pointed to a Marathon station a couple miles away that sold shirts. I'm certain that they only sold them because of people like me who couldn't read instructions. And $15 later, I was in a purple tie-dyed t-shirt. Thank goodness I'd remembered the no-wire bra. I'll explain how they figure that out in a moment.

But back to the far-away parking lot and back up to the office. I signed in with my name, car info, who I was seeing, his DOC number, and my relationship to him. I get a locker for my keys. I'm allowed to bring $20, which gets turned into quarters and put in a paper cup. My locker key, ID (which I'd had to go back and get on the first trip), paper cup, and shoes all went into a bin, and I went through the metal detector. Think airport conveyor belt. I walked through the metal detector then over to another line where I walked back and forth. This other line had a sensor that detects electronics in case I smuggled a cell phone in some remote location. I got a hand stamped and grabbed my belongings. If you have to go to the restroom anywhere in this process, you have to go before the metal detector and what you wipe your hands with has to be put in a bin outside the restroom. I was just happy there was a door.

After the hand stamp, I wasn't free yet. I got patted down by a female officer. Arms out, she went over everything just like in the cop shows plus inside my mouths and the bottoms of my feet. Oh, and the wireless bras? She runs her hands up under your breasts to make sure there's no wires. If you happen to forget, you have two choices: leave and replace your undergarment or take out the wires. I've seen women go in a room they offer and remove the underwires. Love runs deep.

After the pat down, I went through a door where I showed my ID and hand stamp to another officer through a bank teller drawer. It was five feet away from where I just was. Then she buzzes a door open, and I walk outside and down about 50 yards to another building where visitations are held. No umbrellas or coats allowed, of course, so whatever the weather, you're just in your clothes.

I went into a waiting room to sit and wait for another officer who checked me in. I wrote in (again) all the sign in info I wrote at the main building. Except they didn't care about the car. And again, I have a pat down. I'm pretty sure I was dating someone there by now. While all this had been happening, they'd let August know I was there. I was cleared to go into the visitation room.

The room had a guard desk in the middle. Surrounding that are small cubes that function as tables with numbers on them and an "X" on one side and a chair on either side. Inmates in tan jumpsuits were all seated on the "X" side with one visitor on the other. In some cases, there was a wife and a couple of kids and maybe one child was on the inmate's lap. Those were the ones that make my heart break. I showed my ID to the guard at the desk, and he gave me a cube number to go to. I waited.

August finally came in. He was being swallowed by his tan jumpsuit. They obviously don't make them for a boy/man as little as he is. I was allowed to stand and hug him. I didn't want to let go. I also sneaked a couple cheek kisses, even though he didn't want them. We sat down, and it was weird and awkward. I asked him if he wanted food. I was allowed to get up and get him food. He looked around at the machines and picked out a Mountain Dew, Honey Bun, and some candy. I got up and got the food. He couldn't have it in the wrappers. I had to go to the desk and pour the food out onto paper plates. I got a Diet Coke for me.

We talked about everything and nothing. He'd gotten new tattoos. I hated them. I told him so. He knew I'd hate them. He told me about future tattoo plans. We talked about the program he needed to do to get early release. He hadn't had much of a chance to look into that. We talked about what he was going to need to do to make that happen and how he needed to get on it. We talked about what life was like there. He seemed okay, but I knew better. He was in prison for goodness' sake. He was a child in his mind. He was a child in his body.

I looked at the other families in the room and I couldn't understand how we got here. I tried to play the years over in my head and see where I could have said something different, done something different. Would a different doctor or medication have made a difference? Would it have mattered if his father and I had stayed married? If we hadn't moved? If, if, if...

The only thing I think might have made a difference and affected his life for the better would have been getting his RAD diagnosis earlier, knowing what his brain was dealing with and how we could have gotten him the treatment he needed earlier than at nine years old. Hindsight is 20/20, I know, but that was the one regret I lived with as I sat in the family visitation room at the prison talking to my son.

When the visit is over, I was allowed another hug and sneaked a couple more kisses. He left and I had to sit and wait while he was searched back in his unit. When he was cleared, I could leave the room and head back to the main building where I was buzzed back in, my ID checked again, and I was allowed out to retrieve my keys from my locker and leave. I still had the invisible blacklight handstamp on my hand that the world couldn't see that branded me as the mother of a child in prison. I drove home with thoughts swirling in my head.

This was my new reality. This was my new normal. For how long was up to August.

## CHAPTER SEVENTEEN

# Prison Mom Life

August stayed at the facility in Putnamville for about a year. Then he decided he wanted a transfer because he'd met a girl. She worked at the facility. I think he'd known her before, but that part of the story has remained fuzzy. She had quit so they could be "together" (remember, he was going to be locked up for a few years still) but she wouldn't be allowed to visit him where she used to work. So, he was willing to get moved in order for her to be able to visit him. Well, he got that wrong.

But I didn't figure into the equation. So, one day, again, he was just gone. There were some options of places he could end up, so I didn't know exactly where he was going until he got there. There, ended up being the Correctional Industrial Facility northeast of Indianapolis. My previous drive took about 35 minutes. This new facility was about an hour and 45 minutes away from my house. Now, what used to be a half-day was now going to be a full-day excursion and I was going to have to consider traffic, weather, and a host of other things in whether I could get there at all to make a visit happen.

Then there was the fact that this wasn't a minimum security like Putnamville. When you move from one facility to another, it's required that you have to go up in a security level. The new place is a medium security facility. New rules. When I went to visit, I'd have a whole new routine on how to get into the door and just DO the visit. That should be fun.

The first visit time came, and I showed up to see what was going to happen. It started off good with the officer at the desk having a visit to Terre Haute planned to see his grandson so we talked about what he might want to do. Many things were the same as the old place as far as signing in, getting quarters for the vending machines, locking up my keys, etc., so I felt like an expert there. I put my shoes and quarters in the bin to go through the metal detector, went through the machine, and walked the weird line that checked for the cell phone. I got the way too personal pat down, put my shoes back on, and went into this very strange locked space with a very thick sliding door on both sides. It had the check-in/out tags for all employees on the wall. One door had to close before the other would open. When I was let out on the other side, there was the spot where my hand stamp and ID were checked again and I turned to go down the hall, through the familiar jail bar doors, to the visitation room.

When I got to that room, I learned that no one ate in this room. I was able to use my money to buy food and drinks in advance that would be delivered to August back in his cell. Without having conferred with him ahead of time, I failed miserably at choosing what I thought he would like. Going forward, we got smart about talking through a list of possibilities for food choices prior to my next visit.

This layout was set up with chairs across from each other. No tables were in between, yet we were still not allowed to touch, except at the beginning and end of the visit. The rows and chairs were labeled with numbers and letters and it was a little confusing and much less private. They tried to seat everyone a chair apart, but on a busy Saturday when a family comes to visit, you might find yourself with a whole family on either side. Oh, and there was a line on the floor that your feet couldn't go past, one on your side and one on theirs. Every once in a while, you'd hear the guard say something to someone to pull their feet back because they'd slouched down in their uncomfortable plastic chair and their feet had gone out past the line. The surreal nature of this being an issue in my life now is not lost on me.

Again, the conversation started out as small talk about my food choice failures and the plans for better preparation. We talked about what was different here vs. the old place. Much was different, but there were opportunities too that he could take advantage of. They had a dog training program like he had at CALO. We talked about that being something he could do. He said no. There were horses here. He said no. There were agricultural programs here. He said no. He seemed determined to do as little as possible to better his situation.

I continued to make this 7-hour trek every two weeks, which was as often as I'm allowed, for several months. The goal of this move was for the new "girlfriend" to be able to go see him. That never happened. Her mother got involved, let me know that she didn't like them being involved, and she knew someone on the prison board. Next thing I know, August is in solitary confinement, and her daughter almost got arrested for her involvement with him. I hope her mom felt good about that.

Having a child in prison means you have to be ready for a lot of changes. You'd think it would be the opposite, that every day was the same. But it's amazing how much it's not. August so desperately wanted to get out, to relieve the boredom, that he made a lot of bad choices, even in there. But I took it all in stride, tried to help and teach him lessons, and hoped that, one day, he'd see the value in what this experience had taught him. And I kept loving him through it all because I was his mother.

# EPILOGUE

I'd like to write that this story has a buttoned-up happy ending. That August got out of prison and we had a tearful reunion and everything got all better. But if you're reading this as a RAD parent or family member, I think you know that it doesn't work that way much of the time.

August remains at the prison. He luckily got out of solitary in 2019 just in time for his father and me to visit him in February of 2020 before the prison was closed to visitors when COVID hit. That was the last time I saw him in person. For over a year it was just phone calls. That got tense, particularly as outbreaks occurred throughout the prison system, and I had no way to protect him in there. And he got tense. As they required them to stay in their cells 23 hours a day to keep them distanced and safe. You thought we had it bad.

Just within the last couple of months we've been able to have video visits, the incarcerated version of Zoom calls. It required a convoluted and complicated process where I have had to get approved all over again just like being able to visit in person. That took a few weeks. Then the first night I was going to have a visit, I got ready to log on and then the system informed me that a whole software program had to be downloaded to connect. That took the entire 10 minutes of the phone call. I was furious. But since then, I had figured it out and we've been able to have several video visits. It's loud and the connection isn't great, but I've been able to actually see his face. It's been such a relief. He'd gotten several additional tattoos (that's what results when you're bored in prison). I hate them.

As far as when he'll be getting released, that's anyone's guess. There's a release date, but he gets credit for good behavior.

Now, there hasn't been as much of that as there should have been. And he may be getting into a program which will speed up the process if he does in fact get in and complete it. But that should have happened years ago when he first got there. So, all of that is a "we'll see."

Many of you may be asking why did I write this book if I didn't have all the answers and the happy ending to give you? Why should you take my advice or recommendations for how to navigate the rough waters of RAD with your own child? I'm not an expert. I don't have all the answers. I have one story to share and my lessons learned. And I have much compassion for those who are behind me on the road. But if this book can help you in any way avoid a pothole or pitfall or two that might make your journey just a little bit smoother and your family have just one more moment of peace and love, then it was worth the effort...

Till next time,

*Shannon*

# Acknowledgements

The last thing I want to do is take a moment to thank some people who have been in my corner through writing this book as well as my parenting journey.

First, August's dad and my son Spencer. They have both been through much of what you've read about here. My immediate family: my dad, sister, and brother and my extended family of aunts, uncles, and cousins have been so supportive. And more friends than I can count who've walked with me since the day we brought August home.

I'm eternally grateful for the doctors and therapists who have worked with August and helped him to heal. And for teachers and law enforcement professionals who've shown him kindness and understanding when he wasn't acting worthy of their compassion.

I also have an extended support system on social media that I engage with regularly who've guided, inspired, and comforted me over the years. It's amazing what a group of people whom you've never met or seen can do for your mental health!

In the production of this book, I have to acknowledge my amazing editor Wayne Purdin, who made me sound like a better writer than maybe I am. And Beverley Delay and Joven Delay for their amazing creativity in the book design.

I hope that this book brings you some answers, comfort, and feeling of community. If it does, then I've accomplished my goal.

# DSM-5 AND ICD DEFINITIONS OF REACTIVE ATTACHMENT DISORDER

A. consistent pattern of inhibited, emotionally withdrawn behavior toward adult caregivers, manifested by both of the following: The child rarely or minimally seeks comfort when distressed. The child rarely or minimally responds to comfort when distressed.

B. A persistent social and emotional disturbance characterized by at least two of the following: Minimal social and emotional responsiveness to others. Limited positive affect. Episodes of unexplained irritability, sadness, or fearfulness that are evident even during nonthreatening interaction with adult caregivers.

C. The child has experienced a pattern of extremes of insufficient care as evidenced by at least one of the following: Social neglect or deprivation in the form of persistent lack of having basic emotional needs for comfort, stimulation, and affection met by caregiving adults. Repeated changes of primary caregivers that limit opportunities to form stable attachments (e.g., frequent changes in foster care.) Rearing in unusual settings that severely limit opportunities to form selective attachments (e.g., institutions with high child-to-caregiver ratios.)

D. The care in Criterion C is presumed to be responsible for the disturbed behavior in Criterion A (i.e., the disturbances in Criterion A began following the lack of adequate care in Criterion C.)

E. The criteria are not met for autism spectrum disorder.

F. The disturbance is evident before age 5 years.

G. The child has a developmental age of at least 9 months.

Specify if: Persistent: The order has been present for more than 12 months.

Specify current severity: Reactive attachment disorder is specified as severe when a child exhibits all symptoms of the disorder, with each symptom manifesting at relatively high levels."

ICD Diagnostic Criteria The most recent approved version of the *International Classification of Diseases,* the diagnostic guide published by the World Health Organization is the ICD-10, published in 1992.[2] The draft ICD-11 criteria for Reactive Attachment Disorder gives this description: ICD 11 draft - Reactive Attachment Disorder Code 7B24 "Reactive attachment disorder is characterized by grossly abnormal attachment behaviours in early childhood, occurring in the context of a history of grossly inadequate child care (e.g., severe neglect, maltreatment, institutional deprivation). Even when an adequate primary caregiver is newly available, the child doesn't turn to the primary caregiver for comfort, support, and nurture, rarely displays security-seeking behaviours towards any adult, and doesn't respond when comfort is offered. Reactive attachment disorder can only be diagnosed in children, and features of the disorder develop within the first 5 years of life. However, the disorder cannot be diagnosed before the age of 1 year (or a mental age of less than 9 months), when the capacity for selective attachments may not be fully developed, or in the context of autism spectrum disorder."

Exclusion: Asperger syndrome, disinhibited attachment disorder of childhood, maltreatment syndromes, normal variation in pattern of selective attachment, sexual or physical abuse in childhood (which results in psychosocial problems)

Alternative terms include childhood reactive attachment disorder, reactive attachment disorder of childhood, and reactive attachment disorder of early childhood.

Last updated December 2014. ICD 10 Diagnostic Criteria - Reactive attachment disorder of childhood Code F94.1 "Starts in the first five years of life and is characterized by persistent abnormalities in the child's pattern of social relationships that are associated with emotional disturbance and are reactive to changes in environmental circumstances (e.g., fearfulness and hypervigilance, poor social interaction with peers, aggression towards self and others, misery, and growth failure in some cases). The syndrome probably occurs as a direct result of severe parental neglect, abuse, or serious mishandling." [1] It may occur alongside an associated failure to thrive or growth retardation.

Exclusion: Asperger syndrome, disinhibited attachment disorder of childhood, maltreatment syndromes, normal variation in pattern of selective attachment, sexual or physical abuse in childhood (which results in psychosocial problems) See also Disinhibited Social Engagement Disorder.

References World Health Organization. (2010) ICD-10 Version: 2010. Retrieved December 7, 2014, from http://apps.who.int/classifications/icd10/browse/2010/en#

American Psychiatric Association. (2013). Diagnostic and statistical manual of mental disorders: DSM-5. (5th ed.). Washington, D.C.: American Psychiatric Association. ISBN 0890425558.

World Health Organization. (December 7, 2014). ICD-11 Beta Draft (Joint Linearization for Mortality and Morbidity Statistics).

Source: Reactive Attachment Disorder. Traumadissociation.

com. http://traumadissociation.com/rad. This information can be copied or modified for any purpose, including commercially, provided a link back is included. License: CC BY-SA 4.0

Sign up for emails from me at www.everymonthisaugust.com and get three free checklists to help you navigate school, therapy, and the criminal justice system. Free! Just for signing up!

Made in the USA
Coppell, TX
19 June 2023

18295760R00077